SECRETS OF A WEBCAM GIRL

SECRETS OF A WEBCAM GIRL

A MEMOIR

ANNABELLE T. BAXTER

SKYHORSE PUBLISHING

Skyhorse Publishing books may be purchased in bulk at special discounts for sales promotion, corporate gifts, fund-raising, or educational purposes. Special editions can also be created to specifications. For details, contact the Special Sales Department, Skyhorse Publishing, 307 West 36th Street, 11th Floor, New York, NY 10018 or info@skyhorsepublishing.com.

Skyhorse˚ and Skyhorse Publishing˚ are registered trademarks of Skyhorse Publishing, Inc.˙, a Delaware corporation.

www.skyhorsepublishing.com

10 9 8 7 6 5 4 3 2 1

Library of Congress Cataloging-in-Publication Data available on file

ISBN: 978-1-62087-667-1

Printed in the United States of America

CONTENTS

FALL

WINTER

SPRING

SUMMER

FALL

WINTER

FALL

1

You Want Me to Do What?

Nearly naked, I was in my bedroom but visible to anyone in the world with an Internet connection.

When the webcam turned on, my profile appeared in the menu of available models. Men selected my name and then entered "my room," to view me in my bedroom and send messages. Ideally, members tipped if they liked what they saw. Sometimes this meant I just talked while in lingerie; other times, I stripped, or used sex toys. I considered myself a cyber stripper, and less often a cyber peepshow performer.

"Hey baby," wrote BurdeningDesire.

"How are you?" I replied. "What do you like?"

BurdeningDesire wasted no time getting to the point. "Do you do humiliations, baby?"

"What do you mean?" I wrote back. My knowledge of the sex industry was limited to catching boyfriends viewing porn. At which point, I would wag my finger and tally up one more strike against them. I was clueless as to the lingo.

"I'll turn on my cam, and then I want you to point, laugh, and insult me about the size of my penis," he wrote. Unless a viewer enabled his webcam, I couldn't see them, which was my preference.

My immediate suspicion was that he was joking. Perhaps his real turn-on was gullible camgirls.

"Really?" I wrote as a stalling tactic, while thinking, how difficult could it be? I could think of a couple boyfriends who had been worthy of such an exchange and yet I had refrained from pointing and laughing out of politeness. The idea that this insult could be a turn-on was mind-blowing.

"Yes," BurdeningDesire wrote. "Come on, please."

My viewers were always frantic for me to watch them. With few exceptions, a click to their cam icon resulted in a close-up grainy image of a cock getting worked over like a cylinder of dough in preparation for baking. I considered myself to be 85 percent heterosexual, yet the image of an erect penis, particularly one on cam, did nothing to stir my lady loins. Penises are like people from another planet: they look too similar to really tell apart. In addition, I hated the oozing that accompanied the aroused male genitalia. If ejaculate were rainbow-colored or flecked with sparkles, there might be something worthy to look at. To me, it looked like a runny nose.

"Is it really that small?" I asked. I imagined a slender, hairless hand gripping a quasi-erect penis.

Without waiting for an answer, I wrote, "For tips, I'll do it." And with that last message, BurdeningDesire evaporated from cyberspace. Like so many other men, BurdeningDesire had no intention of tipping. Exposing their fetish to a camgirl was enough to get them aroused and off.

BurdeningDesire was the first of many visitors to my room who had an erotic fetish. He was apparently a "bottom," where psychological humiliation incited sexual arousal, whereas I, as the abuser, would be the "top." I wondered if these individuals exposed their fetishes to the lovers in their life; or did they aim for a normal public persona and only choose to expose their freaky side to camgirls?

Although BurdeningDesire essentially stiffed me, more lucrative and equally educational days were forthcoming. An architect, homebound for months with mono, became one of my best tippers, giving me an additional $300 in Amazon gift cards. Another one of my outstanding tippers was a married man whose biggest turn-on was for me to call him on the phone and say "I love you," repeatedly while he furiously whacked off. I received a marriage proposal from a wealthy (and unbalanced) engineer from Sydney, Australia. There were even the less extravagant but equally adoring men who paid $20 to receive a 99-cent Valentine's Day card signed by me. One of the more extravagant offers I received was an invitation from a Boston café owner to travel to Italy with him in the summer. Eventually I transitioned to the much more lucrative field of erotic massage. It was an interesting year—so much so that I decided to chronicle my experiences in a blog titled Secrets of a Webcam Girl, which invited some controversy of its own. Once I switched over to massage, I was hesitant to write about the clients I'd met face to face and who I saw every week—then the day came that someone asked me to walk on them in heels and I simply had to tell someone. I had no one, so I resumed my blog.

But it was important not to get distracted. My sole objective was to use the earnings to pay my bills, in hopes that the recession would eventually recede. At which point, I could go back to using my brains to garner my income rather than my boobs.

2

EMBOLDENED BY THE RECESSION: A CAMGIRL EMERGES

At the time that I decided to become a camgirl, I was working in real estate. Despite all the office hoop-la, image-board scrapbooks, six-figure business plans, and hitting up every neighbor, friend, and relative for business, I was earning a poverty-level income. To further exacerbate my financial situation, I had acquired a couple rentals during the boom years. Unable to unload either property or charge enough rent, I was always just a couple clogged pipes or an insolvent tenant away from serious financial problems.

I fervently scanned Craigslist for jobs, applied for even the most basic office work, but never received a phone call. In addition, the few jobs even willing to list an hourly wage averaged ten dollars per hour, no benefits, with a strict forty-hour week. I decided what I needed was a temporary gig of sorts, even if it meant stepping outside my comfort level.

Craigslist had a section titled Gigs, which tended to be either unconventional contract work or a temporary position. One of the ads promoted positions for attractive women working from home making a ridiculous sum. I figured anything that offered more than ten dollars per hour was better than what I was currently able to find.

After exchanging vague e-mails with Mark from Digital Lens Entertainment, he organized a training session on Skype for everyone who had answered his ad. It was at least worth my time to hear what he had to say, although he gave no indication in e-mails of what it entailed.

The Skype session was long and disorganized. It consisted of the moderators asking everyone to wait until the end for questions, women constantly interrupting to ask questions, and non-question-asking women yelling at the others to shut up. The moderators were still unclear about how, exactly, we would be making money, but claimed that $5,000 a week was attainable, which led to an outcry from the group that it sounded suspicious.

The moderators said there were two websites that Digital Lens Entertainment was responsible for driving traffic to—essentially, these two sites gave the impression of being dating websites. Our job, which they claimed would make us thousands per day, was to hook guys in social network chat rooms such as Zoosk and convince the men to go to the other sites that required a credit card to enter, where we could have "fun." That explanation took about three hours to get out of Mark and his co-workers. I sensed that they were new at this.

Apparently, one of the sites was promoted as a dating site with a $29.99 membership fee to view singles in a "safe environment," and the other site, which cost $39.99 per month to enter, had "camgirls." This was the first time I'd heard the term.

The task was to arouse the guy with flirtatious chatting and then lead him to believe that if they joined the site, he could see me naked as a camgirl. But in fact, he would *not* see me. He'd see some other girl, a camgirl, and at that point he would have already paid his money. I would get eight dollars for every guy I could convert to a membership. I was given an account with photos approved by me. When a guy clicked my individual link to join, the eight dollars would appear in my account. Mark, of course, acted like it was a piece of cake.

For those women still interested in the job, Mark required proof of age, as well as other paperwork. I completed my forms that evening, then scanned and e-mailed them to Mark. By the next day, I was ready to work.

He gave me a list of chat rooms to work. That evening, I entered a chat room for the first time. *Tease them*, Mark had told me. *Tell them that you need them to go to the other site to prove they are eighteen, because otherwise you could get into trouble.*

I never considered myself very good at flirting, but I also had never been paid to do it.

The allure of spending time online after a long day of work, as many of these men did, didn't make any sense to me. I had a lot of friends who lived within a few miles of me; the need to go to cyberspace just to see and talk to someone that I'd never met before seemed like a desperate waste of time. I therefore expected all the men to be atrociously ugly and awkward. They were definitely not ugly; however, being asked to show my breasts after ten seconds of small talk *was* awkward. The chat room was a free site, so why in the world would I show them my breasts? I was in my living room trying to earn money, not drunk at Mardi Gras. Then there was the occasional guy who would stand up and ask if I wanted to see him naked.

"Not really," I would answer, but there it was: an erect penis proudly front and center, the guy's arms akimbo as if he were offering me a place to hang my coat. I wished these penis-revealers would learn that they would make a better impression by keeping it in their pants.

After an hour in various chat rooms, involving a few "You're cute" comments, a couple of flashers, and many pleas to show my breasts—I was fed up. I e-mailed Mark and told him I couldn't get these guys to convert. He offered another Skype session to address my difficulties. No!

"What about these camgirls? What do they do?" I asked him.

Mark evaded the question, insisting that if I were patient, big bucks were to be had. I didn't like the process. It was deceptive and shady. I thought a guy should have to pay to see camgirls naked, but I didn't like to lead him there under false pretenses. But what was so bad about me anyway? I looked good naked—I'm no supermodel, but surely I was no worse than many of the camgirls.

I Googled "webcam girl jobs" and was led to a site that I subsequently decided to apply to: ModelXOnline (MXO), whose impressive website featured beautiful, young women without appearing lewd. These models lounged about, looking gorgeous and financially solvent. The site offered a model's manual, frequently-asked questions, and a place to apply online. Unrealistic claims were made on the site of making anywhere from $2,000 to $20,000 per month, but it wasn't the main focus. I never expected to make outrageous sums, but I figured anything better than ten dollars per hour was worth a try.

The application required proof of age and a combination of full body photos and a face shot. It was a Saturday and I had the house to myself, with bursts of sunshine coming through my south-facing windows—perfect for picture taking. I figured out how to set a continuous timer on my camera and moved about the house striking poses. It felt weird to be taking nude pictures of myself.

After reviewing dozens of photos, most topless, I picked a few of the best: the ones where I looked leanest, happy, and youthful. Looking back, it amuses me that I took such care to find flattering shots when beauty was not actually a requirement for camgirl success.

Women of all shapes, sizes, and degrees of attractiveness worked on cam sites. Obviously the most beautiful ones tended to be more popular, but I soon learned many definitions of beauty. I would soon find that personality was a significant factor in camgirl success, with the most critical traits being extroversion and bubbliness. A girl who made the viewer feel he was *the* most important guy in the room generally did very well.

Within a day, I received an e-mail from Rob Cox of MXO, who processed my application and enabled me to fill out my model profile on a site called CyberMate. I uploaded pictures of me in lingerie, and entered other information such as my favorite food, favorite book, age, etc.

I created a new identity: Julie James, a massage therapist from Winooski, Vermont, who enjoyed bad-ass sports like ice-climbing and downhill skiing, was single, and heterosexual. I was, however, worried about being found out by friends and family. I was also concerned about creeps and pervs. Ideally, I wanted to be one reality removed from my true identity to prevent the possibility of my bagged body washing ashore. I felt this was an identity fairly easy to keep up. I had lived in Vermont, so I was familiar with Winooski. One of my yoga instructors was an avid ice climber and talked about it at the beginning of all her classes. And I usually got a massage once a month.

The website could also block a specific state or country. I blocked Colorado, the actual state in which I lived, and the states where I had family. One of my regulars later told me that it's easy to get past these blocks by using proxy sites such as www.hidemyass.com. I didn't suspect that my parents would even know what an IP address was, let alone how to hide it to go on adult websites. Parental discovery would constitute the biggest tragedy of my camgirl career, but the longer I was online, the less thought I gave it.

My intention from the beginning was to tell no one, not even the most open-minded of friends. Not even my boyfriend of five months, Alex. With our state blocked, how would he ever find out?

3

PAUL THE PEE PEEPER

For the first couple months of camming on CyberMate, Paul was my main source of income. He didn't waste time with tipping in a public chat—he was a private show kind of guy.

Typically, while in the public forum, a potential private-show patron sent a message asking if I was interested in a "private" and what I would do for him. The majority of guys liked a standard strip and sex-toy show in a private session. This involved *slowly*—the longer the show, the more money I made—removing clothing, speaking seductively, and then masturbating with a hand, dildo, or vibrator. Anal beads were also popular with viewers. Some men wanted to go private due to an unusual request, as was the case with Paul.

According to CyberMate rules, it was illegal to do "public" toy shows, specifically involving penetration. A public show was accessible by anyone with an Internet connection. A viewer of Cyber-Mate didn't even have to sign in. The individual could be a thirteen-year-old boy. In a private show, the person had an account and purchased "tokens," and then tipped with these tokens. CyberMate paid camgirls a percentage of the token value.

In private shows, penetration with sex toys was allowed and considered legal, according to the CyberMate model manual. I'm not sure if that was entirely true—if it wasn't, then thousands of cam models were breaking the law every minute of the day.

Most camgirls were eager to do private shows because it had the best earning potential: three dollars per minute. Some popular camgirls required a minimum amount of time for a private show. If the guy didn't comply, most models blocked him from her room, and he wouldn't be able to view her for a period of time.

"Do you want to go private, baby?" Paul wrote, as I reclined on my sofa with my laptop on the coffee table.

"Yes, what did you have in mind?" I wrote. I always wanted to make sure that the guy had a request I could fulfill. After each private, the patron was able to rate the girl. Disappointing a guy could result in a short session and a bad review, which could lower the camscore. The higher the camscore, the closer to the top the model's profile appeared in a search. A high camscore was critical to success.

"I want to see you come for me," he wrote, which was one of the most frequent requests. "I also want you to call me on the phone. My name is Paul."

Paul's profile stats showed that he had a lot of tokens, so I knew he was a potentially lucrative client, which is why I was willing to call him. Adding a phone to the mix of dildo and webcam was a handful and I usually had to painfully cradle the phone with my neck while my hands were elsewhere. Even though a guy could hear a girl's voice on the cam, the phone was a viewer favorite because it was more intimate, more reminiscent of two long-distance lovers having phone sex.

"Call me first and then I'll take you private," Paul said.

"Take me private and then I'll call," I wrote, adding a smiling emoticon to soften it. I didn't make any money until Paul clicked the private button. Most viewers would do anything to get more out of their private show. I had learned the hard way not to do anything before receiving payment first.

Paul agreed and I got the message, "Accept private with FunkyStallion?" which made me picture a horse at a disco. I clicked "Yes," and he sent me a message with his phone number. I blocked my home phone number and called him.

I was in lingerie and I backed up from my laptop so he could have full view through the webcam.

"Hey, Paul," I said, twisting my body to the side to create a more flattering pose. Any posture that flexed the muscles, such as lifting a leg on a chair, gave a more toned and youthful camera shot.

"Hey, beautiful. Are you going to play for me?"

"Absolutely, tell me what you like," I said, putting the phone on speaker so that I could be hands free and remove my bra slowly. Usually at this point, most guys said they wanted you to play with your pussy or use a vibrator. They loved to hear that I wished it was their cock inside of me instead of an imitation.

"Please pick up the phone," Paul wrote. I obliged. I didn't like the intimacy of the phone. I didn't like hearing their voice up close, breathing hot and heavy into my ear. And I hated how it made my neck ache.

Meanwhile, tick, tock, three dollars per minute and Paul didn't seem to be in a big rush. I liked him already.

"Okay, I'm here," I said into the phone.

"Want to know what I really like?" Paul asked. He had a nice phone voice, nothing overly creepy. He sounded and looked—because he turned on his cam so I could view him—like a typical forty-something man with a hearty helping of love handles. He sat in what looked like a home office, I assumed, because most men wouldn't be *that* bold at work. He was slightly reclined in a black leather chair with a wraparound desk in front of him. A bookcase lined the back wall and piles of papers, boxes, and books littered the floor. His pants were unzipped and he was stroking his penis. Luckily I had only a blurry image of his member.

"Absolutely, tell me what you want," I said, not even fully naked yet.

"I want you to dribble in your panties," he said.

"Dribble what?" I asked. I had never gotten a dribbling request before.

"Pee," he said. "I know it's weird, you probably think I'm weird," he said in a rushed tone, stopping the stroking for a moment and leaning closer to his webcam.

Despite the question, thus far Paul seemed relatively normal. I wondered how I could make it *appear* as if a dribble had appeared.

"That turns you on?" I asked, smiling. It was always best to pretend to be turned on by whatever the guy was into if I wanted his patronage.

"Yes, I get very turned on when I see a woman pee her panties. It must be something from childhood." I couldn't quite picture how seeing a girl pee her pants in childhood could connect to a decades-later tryst with a camgirl while the wife was at work, but his fetish was earning me an assload of tokens.

"Are you going to pee for me?" he asked. "I want to see your panties get wet. I want you to *soak* them for me," he said, beating faster.

I reached behind my laptop and squirted a dollop of lubricant in my hand—all with the phone cradled in my neck—and then I shoved the wet palm in my panties.

"What did you just do?" Paul said, alarmed. "You just put something in your hand, didn't you? Tell the truth!" Apparently, other camgirls had tried this trick on him before. He wanted authentic urine. Excuse me for not wanting my living room to smell like a nursing home.

"Okay, I did," I said. "I don't have to pee." In fact, I did.

"I want you to be honest with me," he said, in a tone as if we were lovers and I was holding back. As looks-driven as men are, I found the majority were eager for a connection, some sense of being liked, respected, and adored. Girls who could fake that made bank.

"I wish I could pee for you, baby, but I don't have to go right now. So it turns you on? Seeing me wet my panties?" I asked, trying to steer the show to nudity and dirty talk.

"Yes, I love it," he said. As he spoke, he began stroking his penis again.

"I want to see you come," I said. Men loved the notion that their spurting penis was a turn-on.

"You do?" he asked.

"I love it."

"I could come in my wife's panties," he said. "Would you like that?"

What would his wife think next time she sorted the dirty laundry? Wowee, what the hell came out of me on Wednesday?

"Yes, I want to see that." Then he scooped up a pair of his wife's roomy and comfortable-looking underpants from the floor and ejaculated into them. Why his wife's panties were in his workspace I never understood.

Despite my inability to perform the first time, Paul returned for more private sessions. Because he was privy to the lubrication-as-urine trick, I came up with another scheme: small capsules of artificial tears that easily fit inside my panties. When Paul requested peeing, I simply reached in as if I was masturbating, gave a groan, and squeezed the capsule. Paul loved it and spent hundreds of dollars each month on these sessions. Eventually, Paul asked me to tell him that I loved him over the phone as he came. He also loved fantasy talk about meeting secretly and making love. No matter what the scenario, Paul always requested "soak your panties." In some ways, it felt like an ultimate low for me because, even if I wasn't truly pissing my pants, I was still catering to an unsavory fetish. It bothered me less and less as I realized how much these sessions were paying bills and boosting my camscore.

4

From Julie James to Julie Jones

Camgirls were supportive of each other. In the beginning, I'd enter other models' rooms to get token-earning ideas. One of the games I learned was the card game, high or low. I'd pick an amount that a guy would have to tip—such as 200 tokens, the equivalent of ten dollars—to gamble a chance to see something, such as my breasts.

"High or low?" I'd ask the tipper with a card from a deck poised to flip over. If he won, he got to see what he gambled for. After a minute, the bra would go back on, and the game continued.

Raffles were another popular way to shake down viewers for tokens. For the token equivalent of ten dollars, I'd offer a chance to win a Skype toy show. I sold raffles for a couple weeks and then completed the drawing via cam at a previously determined time and date.

Online forums, such as Stripper Web or CyberMate's Model Lounge, also provided a way for camgirls to communicate. I was curious about the other women. How did they get into this work? Did they enjoy it or, like me, did they perceive it as a temporary measure?

Some of the women had been camming for more than a year. One popular camgirl, who hosted an impressive forum, had quit her full-time office-manager position to be a camgirl. She was one of the few who was listed as "married" on her profile. I always wondered if it irked her husband to think of her doing toy shows for other men. Or maybe he understood that it was just a job for her. I still couldn't imagine telling Alex. I just wasn't sure how he would react.

The forums taught me a very valuable lesson, even more valuable than the raffle. It occurred to me that my split was lower than that of the other models. I was earning 35 percent of the monetary equivalent of tokens I was tipped, whereas other girls were earning 50 percent.

"Did you sign up through a studio?" one camgirl wrote in the forum.

"No, I just signed up online," I replied. At that point, I didn't understand the difference.

"Do you get paid directly from CyberMate or another organization?" she wrote.

"I get paid by ModelXOnline," I wrote.

"That's a studio."

Damn. It was never made clear to me that the management company took a swipe of my earnings: 15 percent. I was paid through Pay-Pal by ModelXOnline, which I discovered was illegal. PayPal's policy prohibited adult entertainment vendors. One of the other girls told me that if PayPal found out, they could seize whatever funds were still in my account. I'm sure this did not concern the management company, but it concerned me. At that point, I was earning about $500 per week. CyberMate gave the option of direct deposit into my bank account, thus avoiding PayPal entirely.

I sent an e-mail to CyberMate to complain and they wrote back that I needed to contact my management company. I e-mailed my managers, Ben Langille and Rob Cox of ModelXOnline. Ben pretended to have no idea why other models would be earning more.

His comment was simply "weird." The asswipes were skimming 15 percent off my earnings and all they'd done was sign me up. I could have signed myself up directly through CyberMate. After I told them they were stealing 15 percent from me, they told me to fuck off and that they had more than a hundred models. To get the full 50-percent cut, I had to delete my Julie James account with ModelXOnline and create a new one directly with CyberMate. I had to start all over again, but this time as Julie Jones. It was my first lesson in how everyone was looking to screw over a sex worker.

5

BABY MAN

Within seconds of going on cam, an eager viewer asked if I would look at his profile. I clicked and saw a photo of a muscular man sitting in a crib, wearing diapers, clutching a teddy bear, and sucking on a binkie. Baby Man then asked a litany of diaper-related questions.

"What is the oldest person you've seen in diapers?"

"Uh, well, I have an autistic relative who has not quite transitioned to underpants," I said.

"How long would you let a child soil himself before you would change him?"

"Immediately!"

"Would you carry a diaper bag?" he asked.

"Oh baby, YES!" I said.

Honestly, I felt sorry for the guy. Clearly his parents had completely fucked him up or he had the sickest humor. At the very least, a man had put on a diaper, gotten into a crib, placed a pacifier in his mouth, and taken a picture to share. At worst, this was normal to him.

I wasn't expecting tips from Baby Man, but I proceeded to respond out of sheer horror and curiosity.

"Were your parents stingy with the diapers?" I asked.

"Yes, they took away my diapers at the age of two and made me soil myself."

"So you sleep in this crib?" I asked.

"Every night."

"What do you do when guests come over?" I asked. I assumed—or *hoped*—that Baby Man didn't have an actual baby in the home. The lack of an infant, I thought, would raise questions when guests were told to put their coats in the crib, instead of on a bed.

"I made sure to buy a portable crib," he replied. "So if anyone comes over, I can pack it up. But I work nights at Wal-Mart, so I don't have too many people coming over."

Remarkably, Baby Man carried out this exchange in public chat, where anyone could see his questions and hear my replies. When my cam viewers read my subsequent Baby Man post, a few quipped, "So I see you've met CreatureComfort99?" Apparently, I wasn't the only camgirl whom Baby Man had visited and, according to my viewers, he always asked the same questions.

If I ever find myself potty training a son, I'll have Baby Man's profile burned into my memory. If I was too harsh, my kid might grow up with the burden of dragging a portable crib out each night to sleep and finding XXL diapers to fit an adult frame.

6

First Night at the Strip Club

After a few months of camming, I was curious about other sex industry arenas. I had never been to a strip club before and Alex became wide-eyed when I suggested we visit Big Tim's Bootie Bungalow, the only strip club in town. He never asked why I was interested in going; he was happy to oblige and asked how soon I wanted to go.

If my finances continued to take a turn for the worse, I wanted to see if stripping in a club was something I could consider. Could it be better money than being a webcam girl?

The Bootie Bungalow was located in the industrial part of town by liquor stores, storage facilities, and gas stations. As we pulled into its gravel lot, and he ran from the car to the club entrance, Alex muttered that I was the best girlfriend *ever* and he was so proud that I was keeping an open mind. A man resembling Shrek took our eight-dollar cover, indicating there were no specials for the ladies. Other than the dancers and the fifty-something waitress, I was the only female.

Alex wanted to be near one of the three stages, but I negotia-
ted a peripheral bar-side location and permitted him occasional trips
to front-row stage seating. The first thing I noticed was that these
women were not drop-dead gorgeous, which I had previously presumed. They looked like real women and none of them had had a
boob job.

"Look, she has a poochy stomach," I said to Alex, who was throwing down Bud Lights as if they were free. "Her breasts are so tiny,"
I added. Alex gave me a dirty look.

"Why are you saying these things? Why are you picking out all
the bad stuff? A woman's body is a beautiful thing," he said, not
taking his eyes off the dancer, who looked like she had just sat down
in cottage cheese.

"All women focus on the negative and compare their bodies. It's
just what we do," I said.

"Men focus on the good stuff."

If I had known this a decade earlier, I would've felt much more
comfortable in sexual situations. Do men realize there is no better
way to turn on a woman than letting her know the focus is on her
best features?

Despite how easily satisfied men are with topless women, I didn't
think the girls were making much money. There were three stages
and I only saw a handful of guys tipping, often just one dollar. Some
girls danced and there were no tipping spectators. The shifts were
nine hours long and dancers had to come to the club an hour early. If
all the strippers who were scheduled showed up, then some were sent
home. Apparently, strippers are notoriously flaky; the club handled
this like an airline that overbooks. I got this information from the
lovely and statuesque Moxie, who sat with us during her breaks, on
account of Alex's tips.

"Is the money pretty good?" I asked Moxie.

"Well . . ." she said, biting her lip and looking up, "It depends on
the night. If there's a football game on that evening, it's always dead
here. This is the only job that I could find that would accommodate
my class schedule." Moxie was working her way through college.

Another turn-off was those horrendous stripper shoes, which I've read are knee cripplers. The other thing I couldn't imagine was sitting on a barstool wearing a thong. The club was also a germophobic's horror show. I'd seen cleaner bathrooms in West Philly gas stations. Carpet is also never a good idea when fluids might have been flying. Clubs weren't for me; I preferred to strip in my clean bedroom.

That night, however, provided the opportunity to get Alex's opinion on strippers, specifically dating one, particularly because he already was, but didn't know it. After we left the club, we went back to my house.

"Would you ever date a stripper?" I asked, as we undressed for bed.

Alex was very comfortable with his own silence. Usually he stared straight ahead after I asked a question. After a full minute, I usually assumed he hadn't heard me and then I'd repeat the question, and he'd finally look at me in annoyance and say he was still thinking. The silence was excruciating.

"I don't know," he said. "Why?"

"Just wondered if that's something that would bother a guy. You know, having other men see her topless."

"I guess it depends. Is that something you're considering?" he asked, stopping in the middle of undressing. Alex knew about my financial fretting. He could smell my desperation.

"Maybe." I said. "Or maybe I am already," I said, cringing. Alex blinked. "Have you ever heard of a camgirl?" I asked.

"What the hell is that?" he asked.

"I strip online," I said.

"I figured you were up to something. And these guys pay you?" he asked. "Do they have your name and stuff?"

"No, it's totally anonymous. I work for a company."

"Really, Anna? You feel like you need to do this? You can't do *something* else?"

"I can't find another job and I'm not making enough in real estate. It's just a temporary thing. I promise. It's not like I'm actually turned on. I'm just doing it to make money." Alex rolled his eyes, pulled back the covers, and got into bed. At least he didn't storm out, which was one of the scenarios I had played out in my mind.

"Just promise me one thing."

"What?"

"Don't give any of these guys your personal information. You just never know who could be a stalker." He then rolled over and went to sleep.

7

WHO'S MORE ADDICTED?

Once, a viewer told me that he was just getting online to cancel his account because, in his words, he entered CyberMate and became a zombie going from room to room. Yet, here he was, clearly not canceling, and messaging me. I could relate somewhat. I have found Facebook to be a huge time suck. Imagine if everyone were naked.

For camgirls, CyberMate could be addictive. Many women loved the attention and compliments when they bared nipples or ass cheeks. The notion that a woman's body could cause a biological reaction in males, even over the Internet, was titillating at times. It didn't take long for a camgirl to create a core following of salivating men. There was the occasional jerk who called a model "ugly," but he was usually banned and forgotten.

Most women listed themselves as "single" on their profile, although from chatting with other women in the model lounge, I discovered that most of us had boyfriends. The models' manual recommended playing down a committed relationship, and instead claiming a recent breakup had just occurred. (If a camgirl was in a same-sex relationship, full disclosure was heartily encouraged by management!) Singlehood gave the viewer the allusion of converting a camgirl into a girlfriend. As far-fetched as this would seem to the rational mind, it was a common token-earning ploy. In one case, I used this tactic on an architect from Sydney. We messaged back and forth about how much we had in common; he sent me pictures of himself, including a photo of him sailing with friends.

"Oh, how cute you are, what a catch!" I wrote. He was in Australia, how serious could he really be about dating? There's long-distance and then there's intergalactic, which is essentially how far I perceived Australia to be in relationship terms.

The Australian Architect, after a few weeks of discourse, insisted we *could* do it. "Would you consider marrying me?" he wrote. He promised to move to the United States, having lots of business contacts to secure lucrative employment and, in fact, was coming to the States for a business trip next month. He was excited to finally meet and, if the week went well, get engaged! Once again, I was amazed at how a man could maintain a successful career and yet be so utterly clueless about women.

I believed I was playing into a fantasy, one we were both participating in. Interestingly, the Architect never requested stripping or toy shows or anything even remotely sexual; his fantasy was the adoration of a girlfriend with strict aspirations of being the Doting and Adoring Wife of a successful architect, albeit an unstable one.

Once the ratio of tokens earned to time spent with him decreased, I switched my efforts to other patrons and stopped responding to his messages. I had naively made the grave mistake of giving him my real phone number. Giving out one's phone number was a good way to hook a guy in the hopes of getting more tokens and gifts. He began frantically calling, convinced that my non-response meant I was trapped under a large object. When I told him via e-mail to forget about *us*, he unleashed a screaming message on my answering machine letting me know he had invested his time, money, and most importantly his *emotion* and, if I knew it would be too much work, then I should've told him that from the beginning. I never listened to the rest of the message, but unfortunately I couldn't delete a message on my home phone before it was fully played out, and so I held the phone six inches from my ear, far enough to be incomprehensible, but close enough so that I knew when I could finally hit the delete button. And when I did, I went back to CyberMate and blocked him from my room so that he couldn't see or message me. I vowed to never give out any real information again. Luckily, he never called back.

This outside male attention affected, perhaps only negligibly at first, my relationship with my paramour. One night, Alex came over to my house—always *my* house, on account of the condition of his— for a movie and drinks. Alex also had a German Shepherd that he liked to bring over. I loved the dog, but my bed was very small, as in woodland-creature small. After I dallied in the bathroom removing makeup and such, I returned to my bedroom to find Alex on his usual side of the bed and the dog occupying my space.

"Can you please move your dog?" I asked Alex, who had the blankets over his head. No response. I repeated my request and yet there was still no response. Was this his passive-aggressive way of handling my new career? Screw him. I took my cat and went to my guest bedroom, fuming.

The next morning over coffee, I said to Alex, "Do you have any idea how many guys would like to be sleeping with me?"

"I know," he said. Prior to camming, I probably would've been crying in my coffee that my boyfriend would rather cuddle with a German Shepherd than me.

The other addictive aspect of camming was the *favorable* off-line relationships—the ones that progressed to some form of caring. For instance, there was a thirty-two-year-old engineer named Tom, who lived in the southern part of the United States and was housebound as a result of the Epstein-Barr virus. Once he found me online, we had lots to talk about. He was handsome, intelligent, and realistic about what the site really offered: women pretending to like men for money. But here he was. In his situation, webcamming was a temporary diversion while recuperating.

For me, Tom was an excellent boost to my income. Shortly after Tom joined my room, he requested a private. Many times, we just talked. He seemed so *normal*. Our interactions occurred daily.

Tom was also a generous gift giver. When I first joined Cyber-Mate and looked at other camgirls' profiles, almost all the women included an Amazon wishlist. I hesitated at first to complete a wishlist because it seemed tacky. My mind changed when I saw a woman open a couple dozen birthday presents on cam. Another time, I watched as a model told more than forty viewers that she had updated her wishlist because, as she said, "I'm redecorating two of the rooms in my house." She was a top model with hundreds of followers, so I have no doubt the wishlist was a convenient way for her fans to give without CyberMate taking a cut (or the government, because it was a gift).

Interestingly, women could receive gifts from their Amazon wishlist without the giver finding out the recipient's address. Amazon had a system to keep that information confidential. It was as if Amazon *knew*.

Eventually, Tom recuperated and got his doctor's approval to return to work, which ended our privates. I received my very last e-mail from him on Valentine's Day and that was that. Tom's departure was the first time I thought that it might be me who also needed to move on.

WINTER

8

ADVICE FROM MY FAVORITE GUYS

By January, business had begun to slow down, not only in terms of tips, but also in terms of the number of viewers. I was told this was typical of the post-holiday season. Although activity had been low, I connected with a few guys who offered some advice. I had found that viewers offered some of the best ideas for making more money. Most had logged more hours than the moderators of the site. A couple pieces of advice I liked:

1. Don't waste time with "guests" and basic members. Focus on premium members, who had purchased tokens, and therefore had spent money on girls, unlike guests and basics. According to CyberMate, 15 percent of viewers bought tokens, with the remaining 85 percent being freeloaders who'd wait for other guys to tip to see a woman naked. All viewers made the same demands regardless of their contribution: "stand up, show me that ass, flash your tits, show me the kitty," and on and on. I was raised to be polite to

everyone, but by trying to please those who'd never pay, I neglected the ones who actually had cash to back up their requests.

    2. Check out other model's rooms, particularly the popular ones.
Some acts couldn't be copied. For example, there was a popular nine-
teen-year-old brunette who sat in front of her computer desk with
a pouty expression eating cereal, one piece at a time. She was cute,
young and had fabulous profile photos, but unless a guy tipped, she
wouldn't even reply to the simplest request, such as, "Can I see your
feet?" or "Can you put the cereal near your feet?" She'd just keep
chewing and holding a distracted conversation with someone else in
her bedroom while watching TV. How did she get away with this?
She was nineteen.

    Another model used toys in public chat and proclaimed to have
the talent of squirting on demand, randomly using the end of a
toothbrush to squeeze in just the right spot. Squirting was a very
popular request from the porn addicts.

    KinkyKatie, on the other hand, was a pretty, classy and sweet
vegan doing a raffle to raise money for homeless pets. Just prior to
the holidays, she wore garters and red lace lingerie, which was not too
slutty, but definitely sexy and fun. I'd always looked at those types of
outfits when in a sex store, but never really had the occasion to wear
one. I changed my mind once I saw how many tokens she received.

9

INCEST STORIES

Unfortunately, camming opened my eyes to disturbing perversions. I would've preferred to have never known such things existed. In any case, due to the frequency of this request, a camgirl memoir wouldn't be complete without mentioning the repeated request for incest stories.

"Do you do role-play?" was a common viewer question. The first couple times I received this query, it seemed odd, considering the obvious complexity of role-playing across cyberspace. Role-playing was not in my sexual repertoire. I had a boyfriend once who liked the cop thing, but I wanted to burst out laughing when he pretended to cuff me. (He was a lawyer.)

I quickly learned from on-cam experience that "Do you do role-play?" was most often a person looking to fulfill an incest fetish. After I realized that role-play really meant incest, I quickly answered this repeated question with, "No Incest Stories!"

And then one day I was online, bored and curious. I was asked *the* Question, so I played along. I had to find out how these people functioned—or dysfunctioned. They were definitely well represented in the cam viewer populace, or perhaps that was just my experience. I was older than most online women; perhaps I had a matronly appeal that suited the fetish.

This viewer said he liked to pretend he was the little boy and the mother was molesting—not his word, mine—him in the bathtub.

"Did you have sex with your mother?" I asked.

"Yes," he wrote.

Some small part of me felt sorry for the guy, who clearly had not had enough counseling. However, rather than show some disgust or anger at his history, he regaled me with how wonderful his sexual relationship was with his mother.

It was frightening. Could these people be reproducing? It never occurred to me that a grown adult could look back and think incest was "special." Apparently "incest stories" is a Google search ripe with sites catering to such a desire. And in my blog statistics, "incest stories" was one of the most frequently used terms to find my web site (as a result of me posting this story).

So there you have it, it's a freak show out there. Misery loves company; thanks for letting me share.

10

FREAKY FETISH

As a way to keep my earnings up, I found myself entertaining more and more fetishes. It was a real performance not to cringe or giggle.

One such request came from EunuchsDesire. After the introductory "How r u baby?" he jumped right in.

"I have an unusual request."

"That's what I'm here for, go ahead," I wrote.

"I want to see you do number one and number two over the toilet. I'll take you private for that, baby," Eunuch wrote.

I found his use of the terms number one and number two a bit amusing.

"I don't have to go number two," I wrote.

"Really? You mean you can't even try?"

Did he think I was some sort of plastic doll that could have my tummy squeezed to emit an erection-inspiring shit? Or a dog that was cooped up all day and then crapped as soon as the owner took it for a walk?

I spent my days either at my home or at the gym, where a bathroom was within a one-second dart. I didn't hold it and I didn't shit on demand.

EunuchsDesire quickly hopped offline, leading me to believe that he had no intention of tipping, but that the mere exchange was sufficient arousal. This was a common tactic by sex-trade clients. I have read that some men will book a happy-ending massage or peepshow performance, show up to get a look at the woman, and then quickly exit to masturbate in their car. Apparently, just the notion of committing such an act is enough for many men to get off.

11

A CAMGIRL'S GUIDE TO PASSIVE INCOME

Even at my first job at Ponderosa Steakhouse, slinging spongy ambrosia from white plastic jugs at the age of fifteen, I knew there had to be a better way. Passive income appealed to my inner sloth. In my former life, I earned passively through real estate, which became an active and ongoing loss.

Because the adult industry was a billion-dollar business, I figured I only had to tap into a tiny fraction to maintain my lifestyle. After watching high-earning models, passive income seemed the way to go.

Pictures and videos were the bulk of passive income for camgirls. The top twenty camgirls offered both and appeared to have a high demand. Plus, offline tips—the method of payment for pictures and videos—boosted the camscore better than online tokens. I loved the idea of lounging offline in pajamas while earning money.

Because Valentine's Day was near, I, along with many other camgirls, sold Valentine's Day cards for the token equivalent of twenty dollars. I went to the store and purchased a large pack of cheap cards, enclosed a signed photo of me, and this project added a tiny bump in my income.

I mentioned my Valentine project to Alex, who generally didn't like to hear too much about my camming, but he perked up at the suggestion of helping with pictures and a video. Alex loved taking pictures of me in lingerie, so that was nothing new, but I was surprised he'd want to participate in a video, one in which he knew I'd be trying to sell. We agreed it would be best to do one where neither of our faces showed: a foot job. Given the love of feet on cam, I figured it would have appeal, and it also offered a way that I could easily hold my recording camera.

Alex had a camera-ready penis. It was the perfect size—in my opinion—it had no curves or discoloration, and at the mere mention of sex, it came to attention and never ceased to waver until mission accomplished.

With camera in my hand, and both Alex and I naked, I positioned my tiny feet around his penis, starting with slow strokes, and with Alex's breath quickening, I sped up my foot-stroking pace. We were in my bedroom on the hardwood floor, and I used the wall for back support and to steady the camera in my hand. I added a few "aahs," but as one might imagine, giving a foot job doesn't do much to turn a woman on. Luckily, I was the one in control of the camera and of making sure we were getting a good shot, because Alex was entirely in the moment. It was a four-minute movie. My original intention to sell the video fell victim to concern over the idea of me in an actual sex video, even if it was just my feet visible. That seemed to be something that could come back to haunt me.

Perhaps the most creative method of passive cashflow was the raffling off of a rubber replica of the model's private parts—known as a cloned pussy. I had never known such a thing existed, but on the Internet I found an ample variety of places to buy clone-a-pussy kits. My favorite promotion came from an online store named Pink Cherry:

"Once everything has set, you'll be left with an exact copy of your (or your lady's) pussy that you can do all kinds of things with.

Need some ideas? You can make a magnet, a keychain or a paper-weight, for example."

I'm certain that a person who makes a pussy replica already has some ideas and they don't involve holding down paper at their office. I also can't imagine a woman squealing with delight after receiving her kit and then the guy suggesting that they make a magnet out of it. Personally, I like all kinds of quirky trinkets, but I just don't want to see a rubber replica of my host's pussy on her refrigerator when I'm over for dinner.

For me, there was some discomfort with the concept of a man having sex—or whatever you call it—with a wax mold of my kitty. However, there have been a couple times that married co-workers have admitted to masturbating to thoughts of me and I didn't make money from that. Despite the potential ick factor, I'm certain that the cloned-pussy sellers weren't giving it much thought as they spent their day doing what they wanted.

12

THINKING OUTSIDE
THE CAM

I'd worn the soles of my three-month-old slippers to shreds while pacing over my financial situation. My two rentals, 1,800 miles away, were bleeding me dry. Usually the burden was spread out, but recently, both sets of tenants called with repairs to be addressed. Although my camgirl income helped a little, lately things had slowed down.

I decided to take a look at other opportunities in the sex industry, which led me to www.backpage.com. Backpage is the go-to source for adult services and jobs, particularly since www.craigslist. org shut down its adult section. The format of Backpage is very similar to that of Craigslist, presenting advertisements for escorts, body rubs, and adult jobs. I decided to take a look at the adult jobs.

I'd given some thought to what I would and would not do, but hadn't made any final decisions. I figured I'd apply to everything and then evaluate my options.

I received an offer from a Washington, D.C.-based escort service to do a seven-day "tour." The term "tour" sounded fun to me. After a few back and forth e-mails, I decided to pass on that opportunity. The agency only paid for the plane flight there, but not back, and there was no mention of paying for my accommodations. The owner said she would give me as many clients as I "could handle," and guaranteed $1,000 per day. I'd be screwing a half dozen guys a day. A seven-day "tour" sounded excruciatingly painful. After some thought, I decided one of my limits was no exchange of bodily fluids, which meant sex would be out of the question.

Other offers had been along the line of amateur porn. One was a spanking video, but they said I should expect bruising. Redness is one thing, but what the hell were they using to cause bruising, a canoe paddle? Porn maker #2 had a list of erotic video topics to choose from, including being "doggy girl," where I would have a leash and eat dog food out of a bowl. Sorry, I'm a vegan! Another option was to walk around in public naked and talk to people. Wasn't that illegal and uncomfortably chilly? Porn maker #2 also balked at my $200 per hour fee. If I was going to eat dog food for an hour, I'd better walk away with $200.

And lastly, I spoke with someone from a local escort agency, Mile High Escorts. The owner, Max, was quick to tell me that they were not "full service" and, if I did service someone, I would be fired. Full service in the sex industry means intercourse. Max also claimed that earnings of $500 per day were attainable and how safety was the company's top priority. Max was good at what he did. I'd been in sales training for real estate, and he had obviously been through pimp sales training. He had that warm, super sweet tone to instill confidence.

I decided to meet with Max in Denver the next day. It was worth a couple of hours to see what he was all about. I checked his website and it looked professional, displaying attractive women dressed seductively, but not slutty to the extent of looking like mouth-agape porn stars. The site also offered an online operator if the visitor had an immediate need to have questions answered, as well as a presence on social networking sites and positive business reviews. Mile High charged men $180 per hour for an escort, which seemed pricey for no sex. So, I had to wonder, was it too good to be true?

While driving Alex to the airport the morning before my meeting, I told him about my pending interview. I wanted to hear his thoughts on the likelihood that this was a business built on bachelor parties and men looking for dinner dates. He said he had participated in a couple of parties, usually birthdays, where all the guys chipped in and there wasn't sex, but there was stripping. At one such party he attended, there were two strippers, and one of the attendees bit the breast of one of the strippers. The girl became outraged and both girls threatened to leave. According to Alex, negotiations ensued, and the girls were convinced to stay, as long as the biter was kept a clear distance from the women.

The story was unsettling. The ratio of potential biters to me at a party was uncomfortably high. Alex recommended a concealed weapon. Where would I have concealed it, in my thong?

13

THE ESCORT INTERVIEW

I wanted to look my best for Max, the potential gatekeeper between me and foreclosure. I planned on shaving off every bit of unwanted body hair, whitening my teeth, applying a facial mask, and deep conditioning my hair.

I turned on the shower and waited for it to get warm. My tenant downstairs had complained about not being able to take long, steaming baths, so I had begrudgingly turned up the hot water heater dial, thereby causing near scalding temps. I paid the utilities so I liked to keep the dial low. I waited and waited, and still nothing except moderately tepid water poured down that was only getting colder. *What was going on?*

This had NEVER happened in this house. I was naked and shivering in my shower with only my feet in cold water. I envisioned a rusted-out hot water heater flooding the utility closet downstairs. If that was the case, I would be willing to screw a leprechaun.

I sent a text to the downstairs tenant asking if I could take a look at the hot water heater because there was no hot water. Sending a text might seem strange, considering I could have practically whispered through the vents to speak with her, but I liked to maintain the illusion of the boundary-respecting landlord. She sent a text back: "Sorry! I have friends in town and four people just took showers." I guessed that was who'd come barreling home, giddy and drunk at 3 a.m.

In the Peace Corps, I took cold showers all the time, but that was in a tropical country where I was hot all day. I was cold inside my house even with a fleece on, but time was short, so I downgraded my attention-to-detail shower to a sponge bath and an under-the-spigot shampoo. I had so many goose bumps it was a wonder I didn't shave off half my skin.

The long drive to the Mile High City gave me enough time to run through every conceivable doomsday scenario, while simultaneously picking at the dried soap on my scalp. I envisioned pulling into a strip mall, consumed by bail bondsmen and paycheck-cashing stores, and being greeted by a sweaty man in a grimy back office. So I was relieved when my GPS led me to a building in a nice neighborhood, dormant, but promising landscaping, and free parking out front.

Max was kind of sexy, not in a Harlequin cover sort of way, but more like he wouldn't need to post phony ads to get girls into his office. The space was clean, freshly painted, and nearly barren. Apparently they had just moved there. Non-model type women buzzed about the room, printing things and making phone calls.

Max had definitely graduated summa cum laude from pimp school. His demeanor was warm and straightforward; he kept his eyes from rolling all over my body, and he refrained from bullshit sales pitches. I liked him right away.

(Incidentally, I appreciated all the feedback I'd gotten from my blog readers regarding whether a guy would pay $180 per hour just for company and not for sex. The consensus was that it was highly unlikely. At the time, I figured I might look back on this and wonder why I was so naïve, but in the interview I believed that Max's company truly promoted a no-sex arrangement, which was good because I was sticking to my "no bodily fluids" rule.)

Once Max had introduced himself, he led me into a small, burgundy-painted office where he sat behind a desk with a computer, while I sat in a chair on the opposite side. Max reiterated that his company was not full service, safety was their top priority, and other generalities that caused my mind to wander. Max kept asking me if I had any questions.

"So, how do you screen these guys?" I asked.

"I'll get to that later," Max said, ignoring my first of many questions, and then went back to big-picture topics like creating my own wealth and destiny. It took me back to my days in real estate seminars for newbies. Sales techniques rarely vary, whether you're hawking a house or your boobies.

Max gave me a handout on Mile High's expectations of their girls.

"Take a careful read of that," he said. "You'll need to make sure your nails are done, including feet. No sweatpants or torn jeans. Your bra and panties need to match."

"Match?" I asked. I always felt matching bras and panties were strictly for lingerie models. Did Max know how expensive a supportive bra was? I wasn't enormous, but I couldn't pull a flimsy bra off the rack at the dollar store, either.

Max seemed perplexed by my question. "Matching, yes, your bras and panties match, don't they?" he asked, looking like the notion of walking out the door without matching undergarments was akin to wearing mismatched shoes.

Pretty much never.

"Of course!" I said.

"I would hope so," he said, referring back to his list of key points. "It's important to understand that we don't offer anything illegal. No hand jobs, blow jobs, kissing, or toy shows with penetration." The mention of any one of these words at my prior job between employee and employer would've constituted dismissal, while here Max was discussing it as casually as an employer would go over the retirement program. "If you do any of those things, you can be charged with prostitution. Now, with that said, you still have a lot of options of what you can do and what's legal. You can do a strip tease, role-play, a lap dance, shower with him, dominate him, and he can jerk off while looking at you. You can even put your hand over his hand and guide it while he services himself, but by no means can you masturbate him."

"I can put my hand over his while he masturbates and that's not prostitution?" I asked. I wasn't sure where Max was getting his information. Legal precedent? Max didn't seem the type to have studied case law in his spare time. Chances seemed slim that prostitution was a hand-width buffer from an erect penis.

Although Max kept asking if I had questions, even while maintaining a tone of sincerity, his answer was always that he would get to it. Then he rambled for so long that I had forgotten my question was never answered. The room was warm and I was getting drowsy.

Just as my neck was getting sore from nodding in agreement for an hour, Max told me he'd train me that day and arrange my schedule. He then proceeded to put a stack of papers in front of me to sign, including a W-2. I was enrolled? It was the closest I'd gotten to being hired in the past two years.

14

Escort Training

While I was sitting in Max's office, he told me there were seven crucial steps to becoming a "top performer" with Mile High Escorts. According to him, if I polished those steps, I could be making thousands per week and could go to work as quickly as this week.

Step 1:   Greet the Client

A greeting, to me, involves a firm hand shake and a warm smile. However, as an aspiring "top performer," it was quite different. Greeting the client entails practically leaping into his arms the very moment he opens the door. After explaining what he wanted me to do, Max suggested we role-play. Standing on the other side of the office door, I would play the client while Max would pretend to be the "performer." I really did not want to open the door when he knocked. Clearly, I don't have the ideal "performer" attitude. But when I opened the door, Max gave me a hearty embrace, kissed me on the cheek, and then held my hand.

Step 2:   Cut to the Chase

This step amounted to, "Let's get the payment out of the way, babe, so we can have FUN!" Mile High Escorts took credit cards, which led me to believe that this organization wasn't a sham. I was expected to do the "drop" by 3 p.m. the next day so that the funds I had collected the previous evening would be available to the company the next business day. The term "drop" consisted of going to a bank where Mile High Escorts had an account and depositing cash and credit card receipts.

Step 3:   A Sense of Security

Again, the idea of an operator on call made the business seem credible. It also informed the client that someone knew my immediate whereabouts, according to Max, just in case the client had aspirations of surreptitiously stuffing me in a body bag.

I was told that when I arrived, while inside the client's home or hotel, I needed to place the call to the operator. And then once I left the appointment, I needed to call to let them know I had safely left.

In the event that the operator did not hear from me after an hour-long appointment, they would call me. If I repeatedly failed to respond to the phone call, Max claimed that they would call the police.

"How often does this happen?" I asked Max.

"Never," he said dismissively before he went on to Step 4.

Step 4:   Check for Guns, Knives, Video Equipment, and Open Laptops

When Max got to this step, I recalled his evasiveness regarding the screening process. A gun? Really? After hearing this, I began reevaluating my judgment. Max ensured me that in their fourteen years of business and their 1.5 million dollars in sales last year, they absolutely had never had a problem with violent clients. That meant nothing, though, because there was still always that off chance it *could* happen. Needless to say, no one ever wanted to be that girl if and when it did. This step was meant to be done in a casual, "Please show me your house, Big Boy," sort of way.

Since nearly all computers are video enabled these days, I was told to close any laptops to prevent recording activities.

Step 5: Converse and Engage

"Take some time to get to know your client," Max said. "Sit in his lap while you talk to him."

Reserving very little of the conversation to talk about myself, Max suggested I ask about fetishes and other sexual desires. Personally, it seemed a little misleading to ask a guy if he likes a girl to ride him cowgirl if there wasn't going to be any sex involved, but I went along with it.

Max felt it would be most effective to role-play this segment of training just like the other steps. In order to have more space, we shifted from his office to the conference room. I found myself sitting on Max's lap, within inches of his member and constantly flapping jaws. It was a weird transition from interviewer to "horny guy willing to fork over $180 just for a woman to sit on his lap." I did it, though. If I couldn't do Max, who wasn't bad-looking or foul-smelling, how could I be willing to take any call that the operator sent me?

"Do you like my ass?" I asked Max, rubbing his chest and pulling my fingers through his scalp.

"Absolutely, I'm an ass man," he said, taking the opportunity to take a good look.

"Do you want to see more?" I whispered in his ear. I then gave a pretend and halfhearted lap dance. I had no lap-dancing experience. My attire for the day consisted of gray wool pants, black heels, and a heavy sweater. Only my hands and face were showing some skin. Apparently, though, men have a great imagination. While I was sitting on Max's lap, I thought perhaps I felt a twitch or two. Maybe it was his cell phone vibrating? I jumped up and suggested we move on to the next step.

Step 6: Undress the Client

Max told me to disrobe the client and linger around his genitals while I took his pants off, although I wouldn't be giving him a blow job. At this point, I could allow the client to undress me (no thanks) or do a striptease. Thankfully, this was one step Max did not have me role play.

Step 7:   Body Rub

Max pulled out a yoga mat (a purity now soiled to me) and told me it was best to have the client start on his stomach. I was instructed to bring a "goody bag" to my sessions containing massage oils, candles, sanitary wipes (!), a feather, a dominatrix outfit, and some games. I assumed by "games" he did not mean Scattergories.

I lay face down on the yoga mat as Max rubbed me all over with his hands. With my face smashed against the mat, he couldn't see my look of horror. He instructed me to make sure I paid close attention to everywhere, the butt, thighs, etc. When I got up, he said he wanted me to do him. He suggested that I sit on his back like I was riding a pony and nuzzle my face into his neck while whispering dirty talk into his ear—and suggest to the client that he should extend our visit, thus charging him an extra $180.

After I had felt up Max, whispered into his ear, flicked my hair into his face, and ridden him like a toddler on a Great Dane, I got up and said I had Step 7 down pat. When Max stood up, his dress pants were jutting out so far that, in the right light, he could have cast a sailboat shadow on the wall. It was a bit difficult to ignore the monstrosity in Max's pants. Talk about the elephant trunk in the room. Unfortunately, Max suggested that we go through Steps 5 and 7 again. We did. His pants did not deflate and I became terrified that a wet spot would appear as I was sitting on his lap. My rule: No bodily fluids!

I was surprised that Max got all worked up because I figured he trained girls all week, year after year. You'd think it would become mundane in the way a gynecologist doesn't get turned on by giving a pelvic exam. Or, I hope he doesn't.

Max finally acknowledged his state. "You are going to do well in this business. You have a sexy aura about you. I'm turned on and that's hard to do."

Two hours after meeting Max for the first time, I was officially added to the roster as a Mile High Escort.

15

THE ON-CALL CALL GIRL

Mile High Escorts required twenty-five hours of on-call duty per week. During these scheduled hours, Mile High's operator called and the girl was required to arrive at the guy's house within 45 minutes, with hair, fingernails, toenails, and makeup done, body scent applied, and goody bag in hand (e.g., dominatrix outfit, candles, sanitary wipes, massage oils, etc).

Max had assured me that the two previous girls he had hired made $500 on their first day of work. "I'll get your ads posted and you'll be rocking and rolling by tomorrow," he said.

The day after my interview, I was on call from 10 a.m. to 5 p.m. Primped, ready, and periodically refreshing my memory with Max's seven golden steps, I waited at home, reluctant to do anything that would mess up my makeup (gym) or cause me to be more than forty-five minutes late (grocery shopping).

I was able to work on some freelance work, but I still felt tied down. Wasn't the main benefit of self-employment not having to answer to a boss? Mile High might have categorized me as an independent contractor, but they certainly had their share of rules, one of them being a twenty-five dollar fine for being late to a customer.

Five o'clock came and went without any calls from the operator. What a waste of my makeup and matching lingerie. Max sent me a text asking me how my day went and if he needed to explain how to do the drop. Obviously, there was little communication between the operators and Max. He assured me that it would pick up.

In the interim, I spoke with Alex about the interview, Max, and being on-call. Although he was trying to be supportive because he knew my financial situation, he felt it was really dangerous. He had been okay with me doing webcam work; he wasn't thrilled, but he accepted it. In-person sex work was a completely different—and alienating—situation for him. I had initially believed my foray into sex work would be online and impersonal, and now I found myself on-call for an escort agency. I was taking bigger risks and questioned my state of mind.

Alex pleaded with me to get some bear mace (in case of hairy, obese men?) to bring to appointments. Like me, he found it hard to believe that a guy wouldn't expect sex at that price or that unwanted advances wouldn't occur after a naked lap dance and rub down. He also suggested that I find the ad that Max was promoting so I would have an idea of what a guy might have in mind.

I called Max and he was reluctant to tell me where they advertised. "Why don't you just tell me?" I asked again after Max tried stalling.

"I don't want to tell you because I'm afraid you'll use our system to go out on your own," he said, sheepishly. "Ok, fine, Backpage."

Here is what the ad said, listed under the *Escort* section, verbatim:

Sexy Eyes, Cute Face, Slender Body, Mature Melissa - 30

*Hi my name is **Melissa** . . . and Toned to PERFECTION. Blessed with a petite figure, striking looks I am truly irresistible. A fun and confident lady with a romantic and passionate side. I definitely have that "something very special" quality. I enjoy the company of mature* *gentlemen, those who are respectable and sincere. Break away from the repetitive routine and indulge in something exceptional*

CALL xxx-xxx-1440

5'1 110lbs 32B/26/33 I'm German and Irish and very fun!

3pm to 11pm tonight

Poster's age: 30

I'd like to mention, however, I am not 110 lbs! Max added ten pounds to my weight, indicating that perhaps he either thought I was too skinny or was lying about my weight. There is no quicker route to pissing off a woman than adding ten pounds to her weight, even if it is just on her fictional persona.

My next reaction to the ad was that if I were a horny guy, I would think, "This chick is going to fuck me." I didn't want to be the one to have to break it to him, that unfortunately I was not going to screw him for money.

I didn't understand. They had been in business for fourteen years, catering to allegedly thousands of clients, yet still solely relied on an ad in Backpage. Why couldn't they simply e-mail their clients informing them that they had a new girl?

I asked Max about that and he went in circles around my question. It later became apparent to me that the success of their business was built entirely on one-timing people. The majority of men who paid $180 for an "escort" and didn't get a hand job weren't likely to book again. I later discovered that Mile High Escorts received terrible reviews from the local sex provider forum. I was naïve at the time I had interviewed with Max and assumed that men were truly satisfied with what they had to offer.

Another question I had was how they could screen clients if they would likely be first-time customers. Max hemmed and hawed once again and just kept mentioning a seven-point system.

"Yes, what is the system, though? Background check? What?" I could tell I was getting on Max's nerves, that our honeymoon-boner phase was over, but I really had to know. After pressing him, Max said that they made sure there wasn't a party there, which, as far as I could tell, involved just making sure there wasn't a lot of background noise. He also said they Googled the property. Hello? I could do those things myself. Max was taking 55 percent of my earnings. He had damn well better be doing something more than posting a $1 Backpage ad and telling the operator to make sure the background was nothing more than a blaring TV and a parrot mimicking the mutterings of a sexually aroused man with $180 to drop.

Max sensed that I thought his verification system sucked, and when I pressed him even further, he said, just as he did with the ads, that he didn't want to tell me because I could go out and do it on my own. Information on screening for an escort appointment was readily available on the Internet. Many escorts required references or membership in a pre-screening service such as Preferred 411. I wanted Max to assure me his company had similar policies in place. It was my safety at risk, not his.

Despite Max's failure to address my safety concerns, I decided to move forward at this point and give it a try. My only justification was that I was broke, with no other income prospects, and I couldn't get Max's claims of $500 per day out of my mind.

16

DAY 2 ON CALL FOR MILE HIGH ESCORTS

Day 1 of being on call was a complete waste of makeup and hair straightener. Max promised that on Day 2 I'd be able to "knock it out of the park," which was somewhat believable considering I would be working more evening hours, specifically 3 p.m. to 11 p.m.

My day was busy from the beginning with a real estate project that had come up. I received a call from my boss in the morning that required me to haul ass to the sticks of Colorado to inspect a government-owned foreclosure. I had fewer than twenty-four hours to go to the property, take photos, and file a report.

By 9:30 p.m., I had finished my report and was relaxing on the sofa with a glass of wine, just as it had started to snow. Mile High called. Fuck it, I wasn't driving anywhere, particularly not late at night, so I didn't bother to answer the call. I just didn't have the energy to tell them to find someone else and listen to their attitude. The next day I got a frantic set of texts from Max asking what was up. I told him I quit. I wasn't going to sit around for twenty-five hours a week to get one call to show up at a guy's house, one who likely expects sex, only to make $80. I didn't even bring up the issue of safety once again, because I had heard all of Max's rehearsed safety one-liners, and frankly I didn't believe him. I could come up with a better plan to make more money. I decided it was back to the cam!

17

SO MUCH FOR NO BODILY FLUIDS

A couple days earlier, one of my real estate clients, Darlene, had contacted me regarding her rental that had recently become vacant. Apparently, her tenant, a gentle, sixty-four-year-old man, whom she had grown close to, had walked out on the back patio last Saturday night and shot himself in the head.

When we spoke, Darlene was naturally upset and wanted me to handle everything, as she would never set foot in the house again. She had someone handling all of the personal effects in the home. We agreed to get together to sign paperwork and for me to collect the keys.

Darlene's family owned a Syrian restaurant in town, so we'd always met there to eat hummus and baklava. Darlene was a gorgeous, late-twenties woman with olive skin, dark eyes, and long, curly hair. But when my lovely Darlene showed up at the restaurant, she looked horrendous, dressed in a frumpy sweatshirt, wearing no makeup, with half-closed eyelids. Her hair looked like it had gotten caught in a George Foreman grill. I knew something was seriously wrong when I put the paperwork in front of her and she just signed and even agreed to lower the amount she was asking for rent without second-guessing me. I asked for the keys and she stood up, waved for me to follow her and mumbled something about going over to the house.

"I thought you said you didn't want to go over there?" I asked. What I really meant was that *I* didn't want to go over there.

"Are you going to be okay with this?" I asked.

"It'll be all right," she said. "I'll drive."

She drove us in her Mercedes convertible that reeked of smoke. At the house, two women were sorting through the dead man's belongings and boxes filled with videos, books, and knickknacks. One woman introduced herself as the deceased's accountant (and executor of his will), and the other woman appeared to be her friend. I guess he didn't have many friends or family.

The home was a 1960s ranch that hadn't been updated. A treadmill sat in the middle of the living room, and books were piled everywhere. It was dark, crowded, and definitely depressing. I didn't want to be there.

I had left for the appointment excited to be doing real estate again, even if it was just for a rental. It gave me an excuse to put on my professional attire. I felt like the old me who used to kick ass at real estate. For a few minutes, I forgot about how I had just had an interview where I had to sit on my interviewer's lap and deal with the yurt popping up in his pants. A proper job doesn't require evading ejaculate.

I was hoping the visit to the tenant's house would enable me to take a few pictures for the ads and allow Darlene enough time to chat with the accountant. I also needed to collect keys so that I could show the home. Instead, Darlene got teary-eyed and took a seat in the kitchen with the accountant. And then the reminiscing began.

He had been intelligent, kind, and always came to her family's restaurant. But he was also selfish; his mother had spoiled him until she passed a few years ago.

"He never did anything to help himself," the accountant said.

There were two creepy portraits of him being embraced by his mother on the wall, but only one photo of his deceased wife, unframed. Apparently, he had had a successful career in the medical industry, but had quit and part of his downward spiral was due to his financial situation. The accountant and Darlene were angry that he could have done this . . . and not even left a note. This went on for two hours.

I could handle contracts, but not depression and suicide. It's too familiar to me. The Baxters come from a long lineage of depressed brains. Suicide, depression, and self-medication with alcohol are all little treats I will potentially pass on to my children. My philosophy is, "Better living through chemistry," whereas my Catholic parents thought antidepressants were for the weak and that suffering was the fast track to heaven!

From where I sat at the kitchen table, I saw sticky notes the guy had hung around his house. It felt a little weird to be reading his notes to himself, but I couldn't help wonder what a person would be reminding himself of right before he checked out. He had *The Complete Guide to the Kama Sutra*, although he clearly hadn't had many female visitors. It was creepy, weird, and incredibly uncomfortable. The air was stifling. When Darlene suggested that I check out the backyard, I gladly took the opportunity. I went outside to take pictures of the fenced yard: a big selling point for those with dogs. *And who in Colorado doesn't have a dog or two?* I thought, as my heels sank into a gummy substance on the patio.

Had I just stepped on a biohazard?

When Darlene told me that she was having people take care of the property, I assumed that meant—in addition to removing the body—someone had cleaned, as in, turned on the garden hose and scrubbed, after the coroner had taken the body. I know these companies exist because I read about one in *Entrepreneur* magazine. I had wanted to ask how she arranged it, just out of morbid curiosity, but refrained. But anyway, what the hell was that on the patio?

"So, who did you get to clean up the outside?" I asked as I stepped inside.

Darlene stared at me blankly and then turned her zombie gaze to the accountant. "No one," the accountant said. "Did you see anything out there?"

Did I see anything? *Seriously?*

The coroner apparently said that the guy had done such a "good job" (strange compliment), that almost ALL of his head was missing when he was finally found by the neighbors. Wouldn't a whole head require its own cleanup? The accountant suggested that the birds and other animals likely took care of the bulk of it. "We'd be dealing with a whole different situation if he hadn't had the decency to go outside," the accountant said then. The both of them nodded.

And they wanted me to rent this place to a family?

I was dying to get out of that place and climb back into the smoky Mercedes. On the drive back, Darlene admitted that she had been popping quite a few Xanax, nearly going straight through a red light while saying she needed to get more. By the time we got back to the restaurant, I had finished a 90 Schilling in record time. Unfortunately, I had to go back to get the photos I needed to advertise because I couldn't take them with all the floor-to-ceiling clutter. I just hoped the birds got busy before I returned, because I couldn't rent it as-is and I wasn't cleaning up the patio. *That* was yet another one of my limitations.

18

FROM ON-LINE TO IN-PERSON

I received this e-mail from a faithful viewer who knew I wanted to make more money in the sex industry:

Here's a potential idea, as long as you have dipped your pretty toes in the water of the sex industry. Maybe you could go on your own and offer rubdowns, either scantily-clad or unclad. I see ads all the time for that on Backpage and Craigslist. You can list in the ad that it's a sexy rubdown. When potential clients reply, just be straight and say that it's a FULL body rubdown, but you won't have sex. Charge a little extra for being nude or topless. You can probably include a happy ending (which isn't really an exchange of fluids) if you're up to it, because goodness knows you'll be asked. You could probably charge $100-$120 for an hour, or $80 for a half-hour, and set a schedule to your comfort. Anyway, that's how I hear it works (ahem).

If I was close, I'd gladly be the test customer. If I'm out of line, I apologize. It struck me as something that you may like doing. I hope to talk to you soon!

A body rub, as I learned from further research, is a sexual version of a massage. In general, a woman kneads the back, legs, arms, and buttocks of a guy, in many cases sliding her oiled–up body against his. This is known as body slide, and it usually ends with a hand job. Many variations exist. Some women don't offer a hand job. Some are fully dressed, some are topless, and others offered fully nude.

In most cases, body-rub girls are not licensed masseuses, and as long as they don't call it a massage or themselves a masseuse, and they don't offer a hand job, they haven't done anything illegal. The typical venue for a body rub was the girl's home or a hotel room if she's traveling or has roommates. A smaller percentage of women worked out of a studio.

It was worth a try. I would institute a limited screening process and only go to their homes, known as "outcall," just like Max's system, but I would only offer the body rub (no lap dance), lower my price from Max's, be clear that I was not full service (i.e., no sex), maintain my own hours, and keep 100 percent of the money. The only upfront cost was a $15 prepaid cell phone, one where my name would not be attached to any service, and a $6 ad on Backpage:

Sensual Full Body Rub by Melissa

I offer a FULL body rub for $120/hr to relax away the week's worries. I'm a petite and slender Caucasian brunette with a sweet voice and intelligent conversation.

E-mail or call 970-555-1515. No blocked calls or texts, please.
Not an escort. Outcall only.
Poster's age: 31

I included one of my camgirl photos with my hair covering my face so that no one would immediately recognize me.

I will never tell anyone, not even Alex, I told myself. To get naked for men was one thing, but hand jobs were something that would likely make any guy split.

Within a couple hours of the ad posting, I had already received a few phone calls, texts (despite the fact that my ad said "no texts"), and some e-mails. The phone calls were usually by men frantic to see me NOW.

"I saw your ad and wanted to make an appointment." I would ask how quickly and usually it was within the half hour.

Most men were disappointed when I told them it was outcall only, likely because they were married and obviously couldn't bring a body-rub girl over.

Outcall seemed like the safest option, and my screening process required their name and a double-check with public records on the county website. And what would I do if someone was a renter? I'd deal with that when it happened. Mostly I was relying on my intuition. If anything, it seemed like a safer screening process than what Max had.

My first caller, Bob, sounded stumped when I said I didn't have an incall location. Quick to get his fix, he said he'd try to rent a hotel room. A hotel room? It seemed so seedy. The more calls I got, the more I figured that the majority of the men were married or at the very least were paranoid about the neighbors seeing a young woman dressed up coming to their house. Bob told me that he would try to "get a room" and then give me a call back. He never called back and I was glad.

Maybe it would be safer to rent a studio by the day or week. The idea of horny men parading through my home made my flesh crawl. After some checking, I was able to rent a furnished studio for $20 per day. This was a higher rate than if I chose to commit to a month or year, but I wasn't ready to do that yet. I decided to try the studio, just once.

My rent-by-the-day, first-floor studio was one room in a commercial wellness center with a dozen other practitioners, including acupuncturists, massage therapists and counselors. It was an old building with a small waiting room for everyone to share, along with a tiny kitchenette. The rooms fanned out from the waiting room like petals on a flower and to keep people quiet, someone had hung a sign: SOFT VOICES ARE APPRECIATED. Most of the other tenants had annual leases, or at least month-to-month. My room was the only one that the landlord had selected to rent daily, probably because he occasionally used it as an office on days when he was in town.

The next day, I received a call from a Mike, as I have learned, *the* most popular name when it comes to body rub clientele. He sounded middle-aged and pliable on the phone. I asked his address and real name and he begrudgingly gave it to me. I said my rate was $120 an hour and he asked if that included a happy ending. I paused, not wanting to give incriminating information over the phone. It was standard in a body rub, also referred to as a Full Body Sensual Massage (FBSM). Mike misinterpreted my hesitation and offered, "How about $120 for forty-five minutes, including a happy ending?"

"Sure," I said. I gave Mike the directions to the studio and he said he could be there in an hour.

Mike appeared to be in his late forties, slender, with receding, blondish hair; he was non-descript in his demeanor as he stood in the waiting room of the studio. I led him to my studio. I smiled and realized there was no way I could have ever followed Max's initial steps of greeting the client. Giving him a hug and holding on to him while we walked about the house? No way. I wanted as little contact as possible.

Mike was congenial and I asked him if we could take care of the payment first. He gazed at me like I was an appetizer, and I just smiled, pretending not to notice that he hadn't blinked since he walked in the door.

With the cash in hand, I told him to undress while I stepped out of the room. I was glad I hadn't signed a lease or invested in a massage table. I didn't want to commit to this business unless I was sure I could stomach this line of work.

When I entered, I saw a hairy ass, the back of his fuzzy testicles and limp penis, his legs with the musculature of a paraplegic.

The only massages I had ever given were to boyfriends, which likely left something to be desired. I squirted oil on his back and tried to make it seem quasi-legit by asking him if he had any problem areas. "How's the pressure?" I asked.

"Harder," he murmured into the face rest.

I did my massages topless, which I felt comfortable with. In my travels to the Dominican Republic and France, I always took my top off on designated beaches. They were just boobs, and it felt freeing to unleash them from the wire and padding they were jammed into the majority of their day.

Going totally nude left me penetrable, either to fingers or dick. Eventually, I began to offer that option for $150 per hour, but it was where I always had my biggest problems with clients.

With Mike's back lubed up, I skimmed my nipples over the small of his back and down to his butt. He elicited a feeble groan. Mike seemed to be a guy who had not been touched for a long time by a woman, not due to looks, but to awkwardness.

"Flip over," I told him, "and I'll do your front." Ten minutes left. I'd give him about five minutes for the happy ending and then he was on his own. As soon as Mike flipped over, his penis sprang like a sofa spring escaping the confines of the cushion. He had oozed while facedown—it looked like a slug had inched its way across the sheet. Mike kept his eyes closed, perhaps to focus on the sensation, and reached out one hand to fondle my breasts like a blind man trying to find his cane.

After a few minutes massaging his legs and allowing Mike to awkwardly touch my breasts, I squirted a dollop of oil into my hand and went to work on his cock. It was a job, I told myself, and not a very difficult one. Within forty-five seconds, he came, thus shortening his massage to fewer than forty-five minutes, but looking down at Mike, he didn't seem disappointed.

I got up to wash my hands and when I returned, Mike was still lying naked on his back, the washcloth I used to wipe him up lying by his thigh. He looked as if he had just run a marathon, or at least driven one. I was relieved, realizing that, in a few minutes, he'd be gone.

He reached his arms out and said, "Come here."

I lay down next to him and he cuddled me, clearly not picking up on my stiff body language. For some reason, I felt I owed him this. He had spent $120 on a thirty-five minute massage and hand job. Then Mike tried to kiss my neck. When I tried to sit up, he tried to push me back onto the bed, ever so gently, and then I pried his hands off me. Cuddling felt more repulsive than milking his wiener; in some ways, a hand job felt no more grotesque than the duties of a dairy farmer. I was milking the cash cow. But cuddling—no. He could pay to have me masturbate him, but he couldn't pay to have *me*.

Just as I was about to leave the room, he asked if I had a boyfriend.

"Yes, I do."

"Oh, okay, because I was going to see if you wanted to go out for dinner," he said as he scooped up his pants from the floor.

"I have a boyfriend," I said and walked out of the room. Isn't the hand job supposed to come after the dinner date? Didn't he realize that he was paying me to perform? Mike's request seemed odd, but the more I did body rubs, the more often I got the question. My answer was always that I had a boyfriend, even after Alex and I broke up.

I was never so happy to see the backside of Mike as he left my house. I couldn't do it again. What if someone were to find out? What if a guy wouldn't take no for an answer?

With $120 in my hand, I filled my car with gas. For once, I was able to get what I needed without worrying about my teetering credit card balance. This feeling outweighed the residual negative feelings from my experience with Mike. I changed my ad to include the words, "No kissing or cuddling."

I'd keep going until I got back on track financially.

19

THE BEGINNING AND END OF
THE FULLY NUDE OPTION

A t first, one appointment per day was enough. One hundred
twenty dollars in cash each day met my daily financial needs. I
still had a modest income from other vocations.

With calculator in hand, I quickly realized that the difference
between one appointment per day and two per day, assuming five
working days per week with two weeks off per year, was the difference between an annual salary of $30,000 versus $60,000. Quickly,
I determined that $60,000 wasn't enough and I realized that by doing
three massages a day, I could earn $90,000. In cash. And not too
shabby considering the work was only about twenty hours per week,
including the time it took to schedule, advertise, clean sheets, and
buy lotion, oil, and prepaid cell phone minutes.

The most limiting factor was my unwillingness to work late-
night hours. Working during daylight seemed safer, and I had other
obligations at night.

My town had a few Asian massage parlors, but not many inde-pendent body-rub girls, and very few Caucasians. The sex industry discriminates, and I had been told more than once that being white was a bonus. I now understood why Max had mentioned my Irish and German ethnicity in his ad.

After I changed my ad to the incall option, I was bombarded with phone calls: ten or so normal-sounding men wanted same-day appointments. Nearly 95 percent of the body rubs I booked were same day.

Body rubs are an impulse buy. Whereas a woman might treat herself to lunch with a friend and a good book to brighten her day, men want their weenies played with.

Usually the guy would call and want to come as soon as possible. I kept my phone with me at all times. I was determined to get my two or three massages a day, and missing a call made me feel like I had just missed out on an easy $120.

Unlike in places like California, where I was told by clients that screening is customary and even expected for a body rub, Colorado men are paranoid, and screening became tantamount to losing custo-mers. I didn't accept blocked calls and I required that a guy call me so I would have a chance to speak to him on the phone. If a guy soun-ded weird on the phone or asked a freaky question, such as whether there were any other girls at the studio, I said I was booked, listed their phone number as a "no" and never answered a call from the per-son again. If a man asked about escort services, I never booked with him. If he wanted an escort, he wouldn't be satisfied with me and I didn't want to deal with advances.

It wasn't much of a screening process, but it seemed the best I could do. As a back-up plan, I kept mace accessible just in case. One time, I contemplated using it.

It all started with my brief foray into full nudity at $150 per hour. Offering fully nude sessions enabled me to make more and have fewer appointments. Interestingly, almost every guy took this option when it was offered. I stopped offering the fully nude option after I met Griffin. Griffin sounded thirtyish on the phone and mentioned that he lived near me. He arrived on a bike and when I saw him at the front door, I was pleasantly surprised. He was attractive in a tan, fit, and unassuming way.

I gave him his options: $100 lingerie, $120 topless, or $150 nude. I hated the lingerie option because a bra was cumbersome and because I usually let my nipples brush against their butt crack, penis, and anywhere else with oil. I didn't want to stain my bras so I usually ended up taking it off, but given a $20 difference between bra or topless, almost all men took the topless option. When I offered fully nude, I clearly explained that there could be no penetration of any sort.

Griffin looked harmless. He was good-looking enough to have had sex within the past few months. He hesitantly took the nude option and I snatched the $150 from his fingers before he had a chance to reconsider. I always leave the room to let them undress at which point I count the money and then stuff it into the raincoat of a toy Paddington Bear. The more appointments I had, the more Paddington's raincoat bulged. It was the only bulge I enjoyed seeing anymore.

Griffin waited about two minutes before he began groping me while on his stomach. With outstretched palms and face down, he attempted to clamp on to some flesh by frantically moving his hands up, down and sideways in the hopes of finding my body. The maneuver was very unattractive, reminding me of a fish out of water, wildly moving its fins in desperation.

Most men waited until they flipped over to touch me, which was usually the last fifteen minutes of the rub and was also why I waited until the massage was three-quarters finished before I asked them to turn over. I let them touch my back and breasts, but never the kitty. The kitty was Sacred.

After fifteen minutes of massaging his back, Griffin took it upon himself to turn over.

"I want to see you. I can't see you when I'm on my stomach," he said.

It was his hour, so I figured if he wanted to be face-up, so be it. As I tried to massage his chest, he put his arms around me and then tried to pull me into him while puckering his lips and aiming for my neck. If he were more repulsive, he likely would have been maced pronto, but instead, because he didn't look like a lunatic, I playfully pushed him away and reminded him that my ad said, "No kissing." Similar attempts had occurred in the past and usually the guy apologized or put his hands up in a surrender gesture. Not so with Griffin.

The body rub turned into a mini-wrestling match as he loosely wrapped his arms around me and went in for a kiss on my lips, necks, ears—basically anything he could.

"I want to be inside of you," he whispered in my ear.

"No way," I said. "You need an escort and my ad was clear that I am not."

In an attempt to diffuse the situation, I gave him his grand finale, twenty minutes early.

After he finished, he turned his head to the clock and said, "I still have fifteen minutes left."

"Fine, I'll continue to massage you, but no funny business."

He behaved himself for about fifteen seconds before resuming the wrestling moves.

"I'm going to end this session early if you don't stop."

He laughed. "Don't tell me you wouldn't enjoy having sex?"

I tried to avoid intentionally injuring a guy's ego, instead of telling the truth, which was, "No, I have ABSOLUTELY no desire to have sex with you." I usually said it was my no-sex-for-money policy.

Time was up. Griffin looked at the clock. "How about now?" he asked, as I got up and began pulling sheets from the massage table. "The session's up so you wouldn't be having sex for money."

I paused and just looked at him. The idea of having sex with him for free was even more insulting.

"Is that a no?" he said, waiting for my answer before he put his shorts on.

"Yes, that's a no."

I stopped offering fully nude, and I entered a NO next to Griffin's name in my phone. But it wouldn't be the last I'd see of him.

20

MY SUMMER VACATION

When I was fifteen, I spent a summer in France as part of a high school program. It was also the first time I witnessed a man masturbating. My summer-abroad schedule consisted of an instructional program in French in the morning and then spending time with program peers and new French friends in the afternoons and evenings.

My friend Amanda and I had become well-versed in the use of the buses and trains. One day as we stood at a bus stop to go shopping, a man on a motorcycle rode up and, with his pants unzipped, massaged his penis and muttered something inaudible over the idling of the engine. At that point, I'd had virtually no sexual experiences beyond kissing, largely because of my strict Catholic upbringing.

What was this man doing? I stopped, at first focusing on what he was trying to say and then I heard Amanda say, "Oh my God," and dart away. I gazed downward, saw his purple member, and ran to catch up with my friend as if she would have some answers as to why this man would expose himself.

Did I just see a flasher? I thought those sorts of things only happened in movies. After he accelerated from us, far out of sight, Amanda stopped, turned to me, and then began to laugh.

Out of nervousness, I also laughed. "Why did he do that?" I asked. Amanda was a precocious, attractive blonde, and had a lot more experience than I did. If anyone would have understood, I thought it would have been her.

"How should I know? Men are dirtballs," she said. "Let's go back before we miss the bus."

I returned to the States just before my sixteenth birthday and never mentioned the event to anyone, but it left an impression: that some men have a perverse need to pull and tug at their private parts while being acknowledged by women, or in this case, girls.

That fall, I began my junior year. I was in the Honor Society and orchestra, and whiled away the hours after school at my best friend's house. I preferred the easy-going nature of Cassie's mom versus the suspicions of my mother, who was forever concerned that I would smoke cigarettes or kiss boys when out of her supervision.

Cassie's mother was a teacher, who was plastered in front of a small TV watching *General Hospital* in the kitchen, chain-smoking in a pair of lavender sweatpants. Her hard-ass father was always punishing Cassie and working long hours that took him away from the home.

For a reason I can't remember, Cassie's dad was home after school. Cassie and her mother were upstairs sorting through Halloween decorations in the attic and I sat on the living room sofa watching MTV, something my mother did *not* allow. I got up to get a drink and just as I passed by Cassie's dad, Mr. Ross, he pulled me towards him and French-kissed me—a real French kiss, as in, tongue and frantic lips.

Suddenly voices came closer, and after he had had enough of me, he released his hold. I sat back down, my knees shaky.

"So, what do you think of this for a costume?" Cassie said, entering the living room and holding up a witch's hat and black skirt.

"It looks nice," I said, looking up quickly and then back down at the carpet. I told her I had to get going and quickly left without saying my usual goodbyes to her parents.

Weeks went by and I never said anything. And then, feeling that I simply had to tell someone, I mentioned to my one of my closest friends, a boy, Bran, that Mr. Ross had kissed me.

"What do you mean he kissed you?" Bran asked over the phone.

"He French-kissed me," I said.

"No, he didn't," Bran said, allowing each word to come out slower than the previous one.

I let it go and never mentioned it until more than a decade later.

Bran's reaction was quite natural, I was told by someone with a background in counseling. "He wasn't able to process the information, so he dismissed it," she said.

Bran and I are still friends. He's a successful film maker in San Francisco, where he has lived with his partner for many years.

Cassie, Bran, and I, as well as a few others, were a close-knit group in high school. We've all scattered across the country, but with ten years' perspective on high school, the topic of Mr. Ross has come up. Apparently I wasn't the only one he kissed. My friends and I agreed that some of the behaviors that Cassie had displayed made us suspicious of Mr. Ross' behaviors toward his daughter as well.

Bran, one of the most loving and reflective men I have known, has apologized for not taking me seriously.

By that time I had reconnected with Cassie after high school. She mentioned a messy divorce. She also said her dad had passed away from a heart attack at a relatively young age. Perhaps it was his stressful job, she said.

I have many stories of broken boundaries. Every woman has them. Perhaps the worst I ever heard was from a coworker. While her parents were out of town, her older brother had a party. With copious alcohol present, my coworker became drunk and, one by one, a few of her brother's friends raped her in a bedroom while the party raged. She was only fourteen at the time.

So when people ask why I am willing to do body rubs versus other illegal and risky ventures, I think back to these stories. When I am "body-rub girl," I feel in control. Men come in with their needy, erect penises, and, if they try to touch me inappropriately, I tell them NO. I enforce the boundaries I never did before. And if he keeps it up, well, Mr. Ross, you'll get a face full of mace.

21

LEASING A STUDIO

It was time to get a studio space, something more than just a daily rental. I had hesitated to commit because I liked the notion of quitting at any time, but it seemed the next logical step. Body rubs were good money and something better did not appear to be in the immediate future.

Late one night, I found the following ad on Craigslist:

$120/month Massage Therapy Space
Massage room available to rent on Saturdays, Sundays, Tuesdays and two additional evenings a week. The office is downtown and is really nice. You can use my table and my hot stones.
If you are interested and would like to see it call 970-555-1212.

It was perfect: good location, low price, and furnishings. I particularly liked the fact that I would not have to buy furniture. I didn't want to make *too* many investments. I didn't want my career to be body-rub girl.

One main reason for finally subleasing a space was an upcoming visit from my mother. As far as my parents knew, I was thriving financially in other vocations. Renting a massage studio would perpetuate the image to my mother of working like other humans.

When I called the phone number in the ad, a friendly woman answered and we agreed to meet that morning to see the studio. Maura, the other masseuse, was an attractive woman in a natural and earthy way, no paint on toes or fingers, but fit, blonde, and warm. I immediately recognized her. I had gotten a massage from her a couple years earlier. She had been running a special and was fabulous, but her regular price was too much for me so I'd never gone back. I hoped she wouldn't recognize me. How many clients must have come after me? Hundreds? A thousand? Surely I was not that memorable and I remembered distinctly paying in cash.

The massage room was one of six below-ground suites (two vacant) with a common waiting area, bathroom, and kitchen. The placement of the suites made me believe that I could usher guys in and, as long as they didn't make a racket when they came, I'd be okay. One of the walls to the room abutted the outside wall, which was much better than being sandwiched between two nosy masseuses.

Maura's room was furnished with the massage table, a desk, speakers, a chair, shelving with candles, and a large bookcase for sheets, lotions, massage oil and essential oils. Maura told me to feel free to use her massage stones that were soaking in a crock-pot of oily water.

Maura and I would be sharing the room on opposite schedules. I hoped to keep communication to a minimum, just leaving my share of the rent in the studio. She assumed my field was massage and, luckily, she only asked where I went to school.

"Pennsylvania," I said, figuring she wouldn't be familiar with the massage schools out there. It wasn't exactly a lie; I went to high school there.

"That's where I'm from," I said, again still telling the truth. I hated lying and only did so when absolutely necessary. It was one of the parts I disliked most about being Melissa, but living a double life required sacrifices.

"Me, too," she said with a smile.

Fuck.

"I'm from the Pittsburgh area," she said.

Relief . . . a completely different world.

"Oh, the other side from me. I'm from Philadelphia," I said.

"What part? I have family there."

Great. And then she named a town within my county. And then another, where her brother lives. I smiled like it was such a wonderful coincidence. "It's a big county," I said. I just prayed that she wasn't going to ask *which* massage school I went to. I hadn't yet concocted that part of the lie.

"So, I have the money," I said, taking $120 from my wallet. "When is it available?"

"Immediately," she said.

We agreed to meet in a couple days to exchange the key and for me to hand over the $100 security deposit. I was glad I didn't have to sign anything. "The less paper, the better" was my new philosophy.

"Do you want a receipt?" she asked.

"Sure," I said. Maura grabbed a tablet from her drawer. "What did you say your name was?" I gave her my real name. She paused, looked up, and then said, "Didn't I give you a massage once?"

Shit. My real name is somewhat unusual.

"I knew you seemed familiar," she said.

"I think it was a long time ago," I said.

Maura smiled and luckily let it go. But, like Griffin, I hadn't seen or heard the last of her. It's difficult to live a double life in a town where everyone knows everyone.

Meanwhile, it was getting more difficult to keep my new occupation from Alex, mostly because I had such an urge to confess. He thought I was still camming and looking for other work—legitimate work. I knew if he found out, it would likely be the end of our relationship, but at that point, I needed the money more than I needed a boyfriend.

22

Walking the Fine Line of Being a Dominatrix

After about a month of doing body rubs, usually three per day, I had my first request for trampling. I have, on occasion, been asked to role-play and another time to perform "fantasy." The role-play guy wanted me to show up at the door in pigtails and a school-girl uniform. The schoolgirl scenario was a popular turn-on, but it didn't stop me from attaching the potential pedophile label to the requestor. The fantasy guy was too tongue-tied over the phone to tell me what his fantasy was. The longer it took for him to attempt to get the words out, the more apprehension I had about being able to accommodate him. I declined to both.

Fantasies and other special requests were much more interactive than doing a body rub. During a rub, the guy was face down for the majority of the session and then when he flipped over, he was still lying on his back. If a guy was a non-talker, I generally zoned out, letting my mind wander and contemplate things such as what to make for dinner.

After greeting me at the door with a warm smile and friendly demeanor, Greg assumed the body rub position – naked, face down, and paid up. Just as a woman can tell within the first few minutes of meeting a guy whether or not she would fuck him, I learned to predict within the first two minutes if it would be a good session. Greg was attractive, pleasant, and wasn't about to piss his pants out of nervousness.

Just as I was ready to dig my oiled-up hands into Greg's back, he turned his head to the side and said, "What I really like is having someone walk on my back."

"Really?" I asked. "Okay, well, let's move to the floor."

I took the sheets and egg crate foam off the massage table and placed them on the carpet.

"I just don't want to hurt you," I said, placing one foot on his thigh and the other over his heart.

"You won't. You can step anywhere above the knee," he said.

"How long do you usually have people do this for?" I asked.

"The whole time," he said. Clearly, this was his thing. I joked that it was a good thing I wasn't a 200-pound woman. He said he'd had a 240-pound woman walk on him—in heels.

My dedication to yoga had somehow developed a talent for walking on people.

"Great balance," Greg said. The balancing wasn't easy. Greg was trim and muscular, which was likely harder to walk on than spongy fat, but I quickly got the hang of it. And I enjoyed the hair under my feet, like walking on a super-soft carpet.

Greg also had a foot fetish. While walking on his front, which included his stomach, thighs, forearms, shoulders, and penis (!), he asked if I would put my foot on his face. Balancing on the face is an art, mind you. I recommend one foot firmly planted on the pectoral and a hip-wide stance with the other foot on the forehead and nose. It's like Twister. Greg was inhaling deeply while my ass muscles burned. I was getting a better workout than I did doing Vinyasa.

After hearing the ins and outs of the Dom world, he asked if I'd like to try walking on him in heels. Why not? My balance is good, but with heels, I used a wall for support. Greg groaned and I left his abdomen dotted with tiny semi-circles. Explain *that* one to the wife.

If Greg had asked me over the phone if I would trample him, I probably would have declined because it sounded too odd. After he left, I was hoping I'd have another chance. And I did. Greg came back to me usually every couple of months and offered a little variety to my day.

23

Ms. Bossypants and Me

The new studio worked out so well that I wished I had rented one from the beginning. On my first day, I had six clients. My business had picked up since getting favorable online reviews by an adult entertainment website. Here was one of my favorites:

I'm a recent refugee from the depredations of Southern California and the dominant adult board there, Humaniplex. Partial to full-service providers, I am trying to exert greater control over my several addictions and malefactions, so, after an arduous moving process, I looked for a feminine touch with a simple, rewarding hand job. It was therefore my good fortune to find Melissa. I'm not a body-rub expert, though I've had my fair share, but I sampled a few local ladies before making my decision to stick with Melissa, who definitely exceeds my expectations in this kind of session. The most salient point is that I have seen her four times in the past few weeks, now, and I will continue to do so. Melissa is a well-educated, articulate, friendly, fetchingly sensuous, amazingly petite, but well-proportioned lady, and she operates out of an easy-to-find, tidy, and commodious incall location. She is punctual, soft-spoken, and greets one with a warm smile, then she gets down to the business at hand, as it were. She's not full-service (I wish!), no kissing allowed—but she allows touching, and her supple, natural breasts and her firm, beautiful bottom provide both the tactile and visual excitement that one needs. I prefer to start with a "happy beginning," and, after a suitable rest period (being in my near-dotage), I like to conclude with another pop. She is most accommodating. These bouts are punctuated by her gentle caresses and good conversation. Melissa is a real gem, gents, so please treat her well.

The studio was also a big improvement over lugging my massage table to and from the daily rental each day, along with linens and oils. Also, when I left my studio at the end of the day, I left Melissa, Body Rub Girl, behind and went back to being me, Anna—separation of church and state.

My goal was to keep a low profile. Maura and I had no reason to interact as long as I left my share of the rent. My clients were well-behaved, professional, and discreet, so I saw no reason for the other tenants, three massage therapists, and one physical therapist to suspect that I was an erotic masseuse, not a therapeutic one. My busy hours were evenings and weekends, when the stream of clients for the other therapists seemed spotty at best. The only suitemate who had a thriving practice was the physical therapist, a woman I nicknamed Ms. Bossypants. Ms. Bossypants' room was across a common area we all shared. If I heard her door open and I happened to be in between clients, I scurried inside my room to minimize chitchat. If anyone was going to bust me, it would have been Bossypants.

Ms. Bossypants was one of those super uptight, persnickety people who desperately wanted to portray a carefree, Zen spirit. She was wound as tight as a high-pitched violin and filled the common areas (i.e., waiting room, kitchen, bathroom, and hallway) with lots of handwritten notes. Ms. Bossypants loved exclamation points and underlining critical words. One such note was taped to the orange-scented freshener in the bathroom. Apparently some people were using too many pumps of this precious bathroom freshener. Ms. Bossypants had determined that one pump of the freshener was sufficient and people were going crazy with two or (gasp) three pumps before vacating the loo. I always pictured her going into the bathroom and sniffing to determine exactly how many pumps had been delivered and shaking her head in disapproval. Bossypants created this handwritten note: ONE PUMP IS PLENTY!

And taped it to the bottle.

It was hard for me not to fuck with this kind of person, such as crumpling up her notes when no one was looking. It was like trying not to pull on a thread of a shirt, even when you know more damage is likely to ensue. The other therapists found it amusing. When Maura first gave me a tour of the suite, she said, "You'll see a lot of little notes around here; they're from Jen," as she smirked. It was in my best interests not to upset anyone, so I obliged. One pump in the bathroom it was.

One of Ms. Bossypants's notes that I had already willfully ignored was the framed note (this was a very *serious* request, I have learned) to please remove shoes and put on a comfy pair of slippers, which were provided. Ms. Bossypants claimed to want to preserve the carpet. In addition, Ms. Bossypants was opposed to high heels. She had posted multiple articles on the harm that high heels cause to the bones in the foot, legs, and ankle. High heels might be bad, but my clients were paying for a view: That's me greeting them in heels and then later in lingerie with heels, not me shuffling to the door wearing a pair of dirty slippers, five sizes too big.

I also thought, to hell with the carpet. I wasn't going to ask my guests to remove their shoes at the door. They were getting naked in thirty seconds and I'm sure, like me, they found the idea of donning slippers fetched from a dumpster or Goodwill repulsive. When I answered the door, I would see men squinting at the sign. I usually waved at the note like it was a gnat and told them to ignore it. Then I smiled and led them to my room. If Ms. Bossypants had known what was going on behind my locked door, she'd have been horrified. Really, where would she even have begun with the handwritten notes? ONE PUMP IS PLENTY!

24

"What You Really Want Is an Escort"

I booked an early afternoon appointment with Mark, who sounded robotic on the phone. Nerves, I assumed.

When "Mark" showed up, he greeted me with an extended hand and a wobbly smile, and introduced himself as "Travis."

"Like you, I have two cell phones and two names," he said, smiling at his cleverness. "And what's your real name?" he asked.

"Ali," I said, which was the fake name I gave every guy who pressed for my real name. It's not that I was afraid of revealing my identity; it was that I didn't want my real name called out in the midst of sexual pleasure. They were not Alex, who was the only man who could use my real name in a coital kind of way.

Mark/Travis was a good-looking man who took stellar care of his body and was probably older than he looked. He was probably fifty, but could pass for early forties. He wore a wife beater that showed off muscles, and a gold necklace. After he undressed, it was clear he spent endless hours tanning naked. If Mark/Travis was single, which he was not, I'm guessing he would've had lots of options in the lady department. Despite that, he was not my type. I'm drawn more to the nerdy professor type—and I know men find this hard to believe—I do not get turned on by clients. It's a job; it's money. One hour and they were out the door and I didn't generally think about them again until they called to make another appointment. I have been referred to by more than one ex as the Ice Queen.

Mark/Travis was outgoing, but nervous. "Do you think anyone saw me come in?" he asked, looking around the studio. "Does anyone here know what you do?" I was used to this question and assumed it was his first body rub.

"No one knows," I said.

After getting the payment, I gave him instructions to undress and start face down before I stepped out of the room. When I came back in the room, Mark/Travis was not fully face down, but on his side with his palm cradling his head. Most guys obliged with starting face down, allowing me to rub their back, though some guys complained it was harder to see and touch me. That's the point. I have compromised and placed a mirror at the front of the head rest so they could still see me, though it was more difficult to grope, gaze into my eyes, or hug—three things I detested. Mark/Travis was clearly going to be a handful and not because he had an especially large cock.

Mark/Travis rolled onto his back after only about ten minutes of being sideways, declaring that he had enough oil on his back.

"Can I touch you?" he asked as he rubbed my back.

"You can touch as long as you don't go inside my panties," I said, when he began to run his hands over my ass and attempt to touch the outside of my panties in an area I did not allow to be touched.

"If you took your panties off, I wouldn't have to worry about that."

"I don't take them off. Ever."

Mark/Travis's explanation of why he was there was a common one: married, but *loved* the female body, loved women, and didn't want to cheat on his wife. I heard it all the time, yet for many of them,

I bet that if I suddenly offered sex for more money, cheating on their wives would be a remote thought. Perhaps not all men, but many, and the Mark/Travis types for sure.

I reminded Mark/Travis of the rules, and removed his hand quite a few times. I probably should have thrown his ass out, but I figured I'd short him on his time instead. I clarified that not only could he not go *under* the panties, he couldn't probe his leathery hands over them, either.

"I just want you to have fun, too," he whined.

"It's a body rub. The focus is on you, Sweetheart," I said.

"You should let go, allow yourself some pleasure," he said, wandering away from my panties and then gradually making his way back. I switched positions out of groping range and watched as his wanker deflated. "You must have unbelievable self-control," he said, shaking his head. Me: eye-roll out of visual range for the tenth time. "What stops you?" he asked.

"I'm dating someone and that would be cheating." Eye-roll again that I would enjoy being fondled by Don Juan.

"Does he know what you do?"

"Yes."

"Really, though, I just don't understand why you don't let me pleasure you. I want to play with your clit." At this point, I had moved so far away from massaging Mark/Travis that only his ankles were getting any attention.

"I know you do. I don't offer that."

"I hope I didn't offend you . . . you know . . . mentioning your clit. I just want you to have fun, too," he said.

"You didn't offend me. I was aware that's what you wanted before you said it. I think what you really want is an escort," I said.

"I don't want to fuck you; I just want to touch you. Come on, you have my naked body in front of you, just let yourself go."

"I think you overestimate my self-control," I said, while his wanker shriveled further. I found Mark/Travis repulsive so I really didn't need any self-control.

"How much time do I have left?" he asked.

Besides being annoyed, I felt a little sorry for Mark/Travis. He prided himself on his hunkiness and I was not interested in taking him up on his offer. He mentioned that he had gotten a body rub a while back, but apparently the previous rubber was not so easy on the eyes, thus saving her from the discourse I endured.

"It wouldn't be a problem if you weren't so darn cute," he said.

"Thanks."

I tried to give Mark/Travis his finale, but it was clear he could only get off if he thought the girl was turned on. I was not, nor did I pretend. That's what an escort does: she fakes it.

After a lot of trying, the wanker had hunkered down for the day and no amount of coaxing was going to salvage the rub. I dressed and walked out of the room while Mark/Travis attempted to service himself, knowing that an orgasm would never happen.

"Why are you leaving?" he asked.

"Our time is up," I said. "I'll be in the waiting room."

Once he emerged, leaving behind no cum-soaked towels, he gave me a handshake. I thanked him and immediately flagged his phone number as a "NO!"

25

AVOIDING THE INQUISITION

It was more difficult to avoid Maura than I had expected. And why did I choose to share a studio? The location, price, and privacy were perfect and the room was only available on a sharing basis. I had looked at other spaces and nothing compared. With Maura, I didn't have to sign a lease because I just paid her instead of the landlord, and the room came fully equipped. By sharing a room, I could quit whenever I wanted.

I had envisioned our interaction to be nothing more than leaving my share of the rent on Maura's desk, thereby avoiding probing questions.

My first mistake was calling Maura when I had an Internet connection problem. During a session, I liked to use the Internet for music, which helped to drown out any atypical mutterings.

Maura wasn't able to resolve the Internet connectivity issue, but while she had me on the phone, she quickly inserted, "You know, some time we should talk. I never asked where you used to work."

Luckily, my client had showed up while she was asking me this question. "Actually, I have to go, my appointment is here." No more calling Maura!

I never got the Internet working and just switched to another source of music rather than risk more of Maura's questioning. Maybe she was just being friendly, or perhaps someone, like a level-headed husband, had posed these questions to her.

Whereas Maura seemed carefree and flighty, the husband was perhaps the fastidious one, and felt she should have asked more questions before subletting her studio, giving me a key and free rein of her professional space. Who knows, maybe I'd seen him before.

Maura's question was a reasonable one. Most massage therapists work for spas, chiropractors, or gyms and build up a clientele before going out on their own. Going topless and giving a good hand job bypassed all that.

In addition to Maura's query, another massage therapist in the suite had asked if I would be putting my business cards out in the common area. I stumbled on that one. Sure, I said, although I had no need for business cards. My clients *never* lost my number once they come to see me.

The other Maura-related snafu revealed my lack of knowledge of massage lingo. Maura sent a text: "would u like to massage trade?" I figured she wanted to trade days in the studio or perhaps offer me an extra day of studio use for additional rent. I needed more studio time because my business was thriving. I immediately responded, "Yes."

A few hours later, Maura sent, "What's your schedule like next week?" That seemed like an odd response for what I thought she meant. I looked up massage trade on the Internet, which clarified my suspicion that Maura intended to give me a massage in exchange for me giving her one.

Clearly, massaging Maura was *not* an option for me, because I wasn't licensed and I couldn't even begin to fake it. There were three other masseuses in the suite; why wasn't she asking them to trade? Again, I had gnawing paranoia.

I didn't respond to Maura's text regarding my schedule next week and then she suggested Wednesday at 10 a.m. for our trade. "Sorry, busy," I texted. "How about the following Monday or Wednesday?" she immediately texted back. I never responded. I hoped if I ignored her, the offer would go away. If she continued to press me, I thought, I'd have to move on to another space. What a shame: I had already disappeared one pair of Bossypants' grimy slippers to the Goodwill. Only eight more to go.

26

I Got a Bad Review

Late on a Friday night, just before I went to bed, I decided to check the local review board to see if I had any new favorable reviews. But—*horrors*—I received, in my opinion, a terrible one:

Melissa is very nice and personable. Her location is very nice as well. She provides a very light-touch massage (I prefer a deep tissue massage myself). Nothing out of the ordinary—but nothing negative as well (except the sheets weren't changed—just spritzed with some aromatic—but I don't know how often the rest of the profession does that. Therefore: OK/Good—can recommend if you like that kind of massage.

Although the review didn't sound *that* bad, he rated me "Average," with other options being the highly desirable "Fantastic," "Very Good," and below "Average" was "Rip Off." Before that, I had had all Fantastic reviews and one Very Good.

First of all, I *absolutely* always changed my sheets after each client! Gross that he would think I hadn't. I had a few dozen sets thanks to the thrift store up the street. Even grosser that he would've flopped his naked body on what he had thought was a crusty sheet.

The "aromatic" he mentioned was peppermint essential oil, a fragrant spritz in addition to laundering.

After reading that review, I paced my living room trying to figure out who it was. Could it have been a Mark/Travis customer who was disgruntled with my limited services? The reviewer had rated a few other girls who were all escorts. The more I did body rubs, the more I wished I could screen out the escort patrons. A body rub was a poor substitute for intercourse. And I was very clear about what I provided.

I went through my cell phone and day planner, where I kept notes on all my appointments. I thought I had found him because he was the only one recently who had come and gone without much praise. So, I sent him a text asking politely if he had left a review for me. I went to bed and wondered how much this would hurt my business. Would *I* go to a masseuse if I knew she double-dipped the sheets? *No* way! And so I assumed men would've thought the same.

The next day I awoke to no responding text from my presumed foe. *Guilty*! As the afternoon passed, I decided to call him to clarify my sheet policy and most importantly to let him know that I *knew*. I also wanted to point out that I always asked how deep a massage a guy prefers. Geez, I had walked on a guy in heels, so it's not like I wasn't accommodating.

I believed it was important to be polite, but by the end of the first message, my voice was getting an edge before I was cut off. I regrouped and left the remainder of what I had to say on the second message. *That'll show him!*

Later that night, after I figured it was best to let it go and reminded myself that I couldn't make everyone happy, I received a text from the suspect: "Melissa, I didn't leave a review. Actually, I had a great time!" What a psycho he must have thought I was. Now I was probably down two previous clients. I would likely never find out who he was.

I felt at a particular low because I had also lost Alex. He found out about my body-rub work just a couple days prior to the bad review evening. He had come over to go out to dinner, and as I was getting ready in my bedroom, my prepaid cell went off. It had been a long day of appointments and I had rushed to get home, obviously neglecting to shut off the phone that rang inside a drawer in the living room. I darted from the living room, hoping perhaps he might think I had just changed the ring on my regular phone. Instead of sitting on the sofa watching TV, in anticipation of our date, he walked towards the ringing phone and answered it.

He hung up without saying a word, turned to me and asked, "Who's Melissa?"

"Um, that's my body rub name," I said. "I've been doing erotic massage."

He turned towards the door. Before he left, he turned to me and said, "First it was the webcam thing, then you interview to be an escort, and now you're doing happy-ending massages. What's next Anna, fucking guys?"

I tried to put Alex's words out of my mind. I had known there was a chance of losing him and I had made my decision—really locked it in—once I rented a studio. It didn't help that I feared that my business, the one that cost me my best friend, might be crumbling from a bad review.

The next new client I got after the bad review was a twenty-something who'd made the trip from Wyoming to have his first body rub. While we chatted, he mentioned that he read my reviews and they were really good, which motivated him to take the leap.

"Except that rotten review. Did you read that one? And I just want you to know I *do* change my sheets every time."

"I didn't think it was really negative. It was just average," he said, bringing his head up to look me in the eye.

Hmm, what a refreshing perspective. I couldn't let the negative comments get to me, not even Alex's.

SPRING

27

THEY ALWAYS COME BACK

After a couple months in my new business, I only offered topless body rubs, not fully nude. As mentioned, I used to offer three options: lingerie, topless, or nude. The nude option came with the warning that the kitty was the NO FLY ZONE. Clients who chose this option (and paid more for it) appeared to be listening to directions and there was usually a verbal acknowledgment or a head nod. But the unveiled vagina caused instant memory loss. Fully nude presented too many problems, those being groping issues. Being touched where one has indicated no touching was annoying, like having a dog that kept jumping up even though he got kneed in the chest. I reserved that option for those I had seen before and who had demonstrated better-than-average restraint. To be exact, three men in my six months of body rubs.

The topless-only rule did not always go over well. Some men scoffed over the phone and others had actually shown up for their appointment and walked out. I was very upfront about what I wouldn't do. Some men either didn't ask or figured that with the cash in front of me, I might bend my rules. Never.

The other issue was my fee: $120 per hour, not the cheapest in town, but very competitive. You can be the best or the cheapest, but not both. I wasn't interested in being the cheapest, but I wasn't that much more expensive than the cheapest, which happened to be a thirty-nine-year-old "country girl" who, some of my clients have said, is "on something." According to the condition of her teeth, the guess was methamphetamine.

When working as a webcam girl or body rub girl, the only way not to feel violated was to be well-compensated financially and to maintain boundaries. For me, being a webcam girl was no longer providing sufficient income to prevent feeling like I was being taken advantage of. When I stripped down on cam by request and only got tipped the equivalent of $1, it just didn't feel good. Body rubs were more work, but the return was much better.

The price scoffers and walk-out all called back to reschedule. I found it remarkable the first time the walk-out made another appointment. He'd made no mention of a previous visit over the phone, but when he showed up for the appointment, he looked familiar. I asked if I had seen him before and he admitted, sheepishly, that he had come and left. Apparently he'd gone to some of the other girls and his experience with them, although the girls were fully nude, was less than satisfactory.

In the body-rub business, the customer did not get it their way. I'm not a McDonald's hamburger.

This boomerang effect was caused by a shortage of body rubbers in my town, or even in my county. In addition to the alleged methamphetamine addict, there were only a couple of other girls, one who apparently tossed a towel to her guests and gave a weak rub in an apartment with bars on the windows. Apparently her sixty-minute rubs were finished in thirty minutes. Other stories I have heard involve sketchy apartments, one-star hotels, sunken eye sockets, texting while massaging, fabricated photos, and up-selling (e.g., another $100 for sex).

I always got annoyed when someone balked at my price or was indignant about my rules, but there was some satisfaction in knowing that most men later regretted their decision. I never regretted sticking to mine.

My clients weren't the only ones who always came back. After about a week, Alex called me. He pretended nothing had happened and then we met up at a park to throw a Frisbee with his dog. It's likely highly dysfunctional to operate a relationship like this, just not talking about it, but it's how we handled my new line of work.

28

WHEN THE CLIENT IS
SMOKING HOT

I was frequently asked by clients if I got turned on. I hated this question. If I said no, then the fantasy was ruined for them. Many guys didn't care if I was turned on—they were there to relax and enjoy themselves—but I generally found that the ones who *asked* if I was turned on, wanted me to be turned on.

If I lied and said "yes," many men took this as an invitation to dive into my panties.

The truth was, almost without exception, I did not get turned on. The problem was the exception, and his name was Matthew. I called him Matthew because he was the spitting image of Matthew McConaughey.

Matthew was a pain in the ass on the phone. He would call, attempting to schedule last minute—as most do—and I'd be booked. He was okay with it a couple times and then expressed frustration.

"Every time I call in the morning you say you have openings, and then when I call back a couple hours later, you're booked," he said.

"I get booked up quickly," I said.

Who the hell was he to get frustrated? Then he tried to book a day ahead. The next day I tried to move his appointment to squeeze in another guy, and apparently this did not sit well with him. He got an attitude on the phone.

"I thought we had an appointment last week," he said.

"You never called to confirm," I said.

Again, who was this guy and didn't he know body-rub etiquette? As soon as his voice got that edge, I felt my Irish temper flare. After our exchange, he quickly corrected his tone.

"In any case, I'd still like to meet you," he said.

I tried not to piss people off because I didn't want someone to write a bad review out of spite or retaliate in any other way. So I simply said I was looking forward to meeting him, too, and we'd try again another time. I immediately entered ASS for his last name in my phone.

After I had an interaction with a guy, I always entered a description in my phone contacts. Most descriptors were "nice," "good," "great," "great tipper," and the occasional "hairy" if I knew I'd need to vacuum after they left. The problem with men's back hair was that it closely resembled pubic hair, and the thought of either on the floor made me power up the Hoover as soon as they were out the door. I entered NO next to someone's name if they called me while drunk, were overly gropey, winey, or sent creepy pictures.

I was shopping at Target the next time Matthew called. I rolled my eyes. Should I bother? I'll admit, I was curious. His voice sounded rather bland on the phone. I answered.

Our schedules finally coincided and he booked a thirty-minute appointment, which was fine by me. If he was demanding, he'd be out the door in no time.

I was speechless when I saw him. I was nervous, which hadn't happened since the first couple sessions. I'd had good-looking clients before, but this was completely unexpected. My surprise was not because I assumed good-looking guys shouldn't have to pay for female contact, it was that guys this good-looking don't generally exist. It was like seeing Bigfoot in the flesh and fur.

Matthew had a quiet way about him, not nervous, but somewhat of an intense looker. It was like trying to look at the sun. I moved on to business with a sweep of the hand. "We'll be in here," I said, then asked, "Did you find the place okay?"

And then he was naked on the table. He undressed while I turned around to fill the room with the soulful voice of Regina Spektor.

His body did not disappoint and I felt that things were askew, perhaps a planet or two out of alignment. The men who came to see me were largely satisfied with my appearance, even though I'm not exactly a supermodel. It felt much easier to please a guy who was twenty years older than I and fifty pounds overweight with a bad case of psoriasis than a guy who could go down to the bars and pick up the hottest girl there. I wasn't even sure I would've been picked and here he was, paying me.

I stripped down to my panties and asked if he wanted lotion or oil. He didn't care and kept lifting his head to get a look, making me glad that I'd recently upped the workouts and cut back on the alcohol.

When a session was only thirty minutes, I got down to business quicker. I didn't bother asking how deep he wanted the massage because usually thirty-minute bookers just wanted the juicy parts rubbed pronto. While a guy was on his stomach, the juicy part was the spot between balls and butt crack. I never had a guy who didn't enjoy the perineum rubbed. Pleasure was indicated by a groan or, if speechless or mute, the rising of the buttocks. Another favorite was nipples between the butt crack.

While I was massaging Matthew, he told me that he was in a long-distance relationship and, although he wanted to remain faithful, he also needed his release. He felt—as many do—that the body rub was a compromise between staying faithful and having needs met.

Matthew had just about the firmest, plumpest ass I had seen, without so much as an errant hair on his back or butt. Every session

included a rub and tug, but how much skin-to-skin contact I allowed was a complicated, multivariate equation, based on smell, lesions,
muscle tone, age, intellect, and how closely the client resembled the
hottest male actor. While I was practically humping Matthew, he
flipped over and looked right into my eyes. "I want you to look at me,"
he said, inches from my lips.

I had made it clear in my ad that I did not allow kissing, cuddling, or mutual massage.

"Do you ever let guys massage you?" he asked.

"No." He promptly began rubbing my shoulders and neck, while
facing me. I was feeling a bit melty and figured, why not? I'd worked
hard all day!

Matthew was incredibly sensual and not the least bit pushy. He
made it clear he wasn't looking for sex, just a hold-over until he saw
his girlfriend again.

While we were cuddling, with just a pair of pink panties between
us, he began kissing my neck, and intermittently turning my face to
his. Although I didn't really want this part to end, I did, by doing
what I get paid to do. We hugged and he left.

I thought about changing his contact information from Matthew
ASS to something nicer, but then I thought about his luscious ass and
figured that description was quite appropriate.

29

I WANT MY CAKE

At one point, it seemed that all of my hot clients were booking appointments, which was unfortunately coincidental with Alex deciding to take a "break." I perceived our breakup to be the beginning of a protracted spell of celibacy, making the hot-client wave even more frustrating. One guy had the most heavenly natural scent at the nape of his neck, like warm cotton candy. Whereas the Matthew McConaughey customer had astounding good looks, the cotton candy guy was the full package. In addition to *that*, he was good-looking with a sharp and witty intellect. What more could I have asked for?

At our next appointment, he put his arms around me, lightly, as I was massaging his chest. I sank a little closer, feeling his breath on my ear. I just couldn't look at him, but his hands and arms worked their way around my back in a way that made me collapse on his chest. By the time I was kissing his nipples, fully naked, with my hands traversing his body, my office policies were not even a remote thought.

A good body rub, one that segues into a mutual massage and kissing, can be some of the most phenomenal foreplay. Foreplay without the sex, though, can be torturous. It's a tricky situation when there's an exchange of money at the onset.

The problem with being a body rubber was that most guys would not be comfortable with a girlfriend who does such things, so the attractive single customers were un-dateable because they already knew what I did. This left me with either lying to a future boyfriend, which sounded messy and horrendous, or having my vagina explode from sexual repression. The other option was finding a Boy Friday, a guy, preferably younger, who provides fun and fulfills sexual needs. Boy Friday wouldn't get too close (emotionally that is, physically YES!) so there would be no need to explain the two cell phones, the constant stream of sheets in the washer, or paying for everything in cash.

I never considered becoming an escort (i.e., full service) because I believed (and still do) that sex should be consensual and free for both parties. I couldn't cross that line. If I began to have sex with men that I found repulsive, I think soon after I would have found sex itself repulsive.

Would I have loved to have sex with a couple of my customers? Yes. I just wouldn't have wanted to do it for money. Which brought up another dilemma; if I transitioned a single, hot client to a Boy Friday, it would've been like giving up the best part of the job: Being intimate with a guy who actually turned me on. These men represented something fewer than 5 percent.

Every job has its pluses. When my roommate in college worked at Ben and Jerry's, she got free ice cream. When I was a bureaucrat, I had generous medical benefits. The hot clients were the free ice cream and $3 co-pays. I guess I wanted my cake and to have them eat me, too.

30

A SURE THING

The guy who smelled like cotton candy sent me a text a few minutes after he left his session: "That was amazing! I could barely walk to my car," he wrote. Sexting ensued, implying another titillating interlude, one outside the confines of the studio. Admittedly, in any other circumstance, we would have had sex. He was hot, intelligent, and witty. He was also more than ten years younger than me.

I didn't care if I blurred the lines of our professional relationship; I wanted to spend an evening with him. I might lose him as a client, but I was single, celibate, and stopped up.

Where should we meet? he wrote via text.

I don't like texting for dates. It's cowardly and lazy. But he was young, perhaps nervous, and maybe that's what the kids do these days. I let it slide. I think it's important to let a guy arrange a date; at best I might redirect him. After a lot of indecision, we finally chose to meet at his house.

He had just moved in, he explained, so I'd have to overlook the boxes and such. No problem. I understood.

He lived in a multi-family unit in a great part of town. We were literally within walking distance of restaurants, bars, and boutiques. When he greeted me at the door, he looked at me as if he had never seen me before.

"Wow, you look amazing," he said, taking a step back, still holding the doorknob.

"Thanks," I said, walking past him.

I complimented his space, although it was difficult to appreciate it with the mountain of boxes. The old building was likely a beauty in its heyday, but it had been subdivided into three units. Illegally subdivided, my background told me: shared air, no easement windows, and a deadbolt that required a key to exit. I couldn't help but focus on the large cracks and flaking paint above the sofa.

"The landlord says that's nothing to be concerned about," he said, pointing to the wall.

"When did you move in?" I asked.

"A couple months ago," he said.

A couple months? It looked like he had just moved in a couple hours ago.

I was getting tired of standing, oohing and aahing over the size of the closets and the height of the ceilings, so I sat down, giving up on him asking me to sit.

Cotton Candy Guy was naturally cute, but clearly he hadn't spiffed up. He was comfortably dressed in droopy shorts, no belt, no shoes, and a concert t-shirt. He sat down next to me and pulled out a photo album, showing me all the pictures from every vacation he ever took.

I asked if a woman in the picture was his sister, and he promptly jumped up to show me pictures of all his family.

"My sister painted this of me," he said, removing a painting from the mantel of the non-functioning fireplace.

The black-and-white portrait faintly resembled Cotton Candy Guy. The neck was that of a giraffe topped with a stiff facial expression, making it seem as though he were being strangled.

"Did she paint it from a photo?" *Like a funhouse mirror photo?*

"No, I sat for her," he said, smiling at his grimacing self. "She forgot to paint an eyebrow though," he said, pointing to the space above his eye, still grinning.

"I didn't notice," I said. "It's lovely. You and your sister seem close."

"Yes, she's in MENSA. So am I."

"I'm impressed," I said. Actually, I'd known a couple morons who'd made it through the rigors of MENSA membership.

I had gone on a long run before I came over his house and I was beyond parched.

"Can I have a drink?" I asked.

"Is water okay? Because that's all I have."

"Perfect," I said. So much for the cocktails and hors d'oeuvres.

"Do you want to go out? We could walk," I said. I hadn't eaten dinner in anticipation of, well, what usually comes with a date at seven o'clock–food!

"I thought we'd just stay here. Did you bring your oils?" he asked.

I paused. Did he think this was a free outcall session? Did he really think I was going to put a bottle of *oil* in my vegan purse?

"I could massage you first," he offered with a wobbly smile.

"Okay," I said. I was already here, after all. But my libido was deflating. Every girl appreciates being wined and dined. He had spent hundreds on me every month and here he had me in his apartment, but had neglected to splurge on a $10 bottle of wine.

We went to his bedroom and he turned on some music from his laptop. "Oh, the lotion," he said and darted to the bathroom, while I undressed and lay down on his bed.

He came back with two bottles: a bottle of face moisturizer and a jug of cheap lotion. I went with the face moisturizer while realizing he probably hoped I would select the cheaper option.

He squirted a cold dollop directly onto my back, giving me a start, and dug in as if he were reluctantly putting suntan lotion on a frat brother's back.

After about ten minutes, he asked, "Ready to do me?"

I went to work massaging him, just like in one of our sessions. He lay there like an invalid, moaning when I hit the parts he liked. I told him to flip over, hoping face-to-face would encourage a little something-something.

With my face within inches of his, he kissed me, which was new territory for us. He tasted good and felt good, but I had lost the passion when I realized he probably felt no need to impress me because I was a sure thing.

After his hands began to wander and his kissing descended down to my breasts, I pulled back and said, "I hate to say this, but I should be going." Doing body rubs has made it easier for me to say no without explanation.

He propped himself on one elbow, trying to find some words, and fumbling for the glasses he had removed.

"It's nothing personal, I just need to go," I said as I scooped my red dress from the floor and slipped it over my head.

I walked to the door before he had a chance to dress and realized I needed his key to get out. Damn those code violations!

"Did I do something?" he asked, suddenly behind me. He looked confused, but not annoyed or willing to press the issue.

"No," I said and smiled, looking at the lock and then back to him.

"Oh, right," he said as he picked up the keys, unlocked the door, and then took a step back and extended his arms for a hug.

I reached up, hugged, and kissed him on his sweet-smelling, scruffy cheek. I lingered for a moment, amazed that I had felt a compelling attraction to him in the studio and that it had all fizzled when I was on his turf, waiting for him to take the lead. Perhaps one of the allures of a body rub was that it catered to sexual ineptitude or laziness. I did the work and looked—and hoped!—for no attempts at reciprocation. I've had non-reciprocating boyfriends in the past and they were disappointing partners.

That night, I regretted my decision to go out with him, and vowed never to do it again. I hoped that I hadn't lost one of my favorite clients.

Cotton Candy Guy eventually came back. Apparently he hadn't perceived my sudden departure as a dismissal of his affections, because he continued to send a few texts hinting that I needed to come back. "My new bed just got delivered. I need someone to break it in ☺," he wrote. I wrote back that I was flattered, but that I had gotten back together with my boyfriend. It was the softest rejection.

We resumed our sessions. With the sad reality of what it was like to spend an evening with Cotton Candy Guy, our rubs were never as steamy. I had imagined him to be mind-blowing in the sack. Once I learned otherwise, my desire dissipated.

31

HIS SOULMATE

I had a client who said I reminded him of his wife. His dead wife. And I assumed, because he was in his mid-sixties and she had just passed, that my similarity was to her in her younger days. Perhaps he remembered her that way.

After he retired, they fulfilled a life-long desire to buy a home in Mexico to spend the winters. His wife developed a liver disease and swiftly declined. Getting clearance from her doctors to go to Mexico with family, her condition took a sudden turn and she died there. He subsequently sold the Mexican home.

"She was conservative, but she had her navel pierced," he said as he looked at my pierced belly button while I massaged his legs. Body rubs seemed a new thing for him because he was bashful at first, leaving his underwear on, until encouraged otherwise. "I used to buy really nice ones for her. Nice jewels. It was our thing," he said, now staring at the ceiling.

It had been less than a year since his wife passed away. He said he wasn't ready to date and, with his daughter moving on, things at home were awfully quiet.

He was an easy client, one whose session went by quickly, one who seemed appreciative of any level of contact. He touched me tentatively, like one approaching a jellyfish with a stick.

He generally came to see me every month or so. Then, one day, he booked again after seeing me just a week prior, on short notice—very unlike him.

He hugged me for longer than usual. Then he gave me the money and, instead of undressing, he paused and said, "I have an unusual request."

"Go ahead. I get a lot of those," I said.

"Instead of a massage, can we get a drink? Perhaps an appetizer if you're hungry? It won't take any longer than an hour. I promise."

I don't drink with clients. But this was the Sweet Widower. He didn't want me, he wanted his wife. Given that, I agreed. Besides, the thought of going out for a drink was more appealing after a long day of appointments.

We drove to one of my favorite restaurants, a wine bar with amazing tapas, located a few minutes from my studio. It was his anniversary and he was having a hard time. He barely drank his wine and picked at the bacon-wrapped apricots.

I listened to him talk about his wife and realized how lucky he was to have had such a love. I haven't come close to that type of relationship. I often am privy to the disgruntled end of marriages. Growing up gave me a myopic—and torturous—view of "staying together for the kids." Still married, separate bedrooms, now just torturing themselves.

When the hour was more than up, I really had to leave. I had plans with a new Boy Friday and wanted to clock out as Body Rub Girl. Sweet Widower got up and I told him I could walk back to the studio. He still hadn't finished his drink or food and looked rather comfy relaxing in an overstuffed leather chair.

He leaned in to give me a hug, lingered, and then when he pulled back, he said, "Thanks, Marie." He quickly blushed and self-corrected. Neither my name, nor any of my fake names, was Marie, but I knew whose was.

32

WHEN I BUMPED INTO SOMEONE
FROM THE "NO" LIST

During lunch hour one day, while I was riding my bike from studio to home, a guy rode up alongside me and said, "Well, I know your name isn't Melissa."

Griffin, the good-looking, fit, late thirty-something, who didn't understand the word "no," was right beside me.

This was the guy who'd turned our body rub into a wrestling match as he flipped me over and I kept wriggling out of his embrace. Griffin was the guy who came closest to getting maced.

I wasn't too surprised to see him again. I knew he lived near me because he'd come to the session on his bike.

"I'm Griffin," he said as he squeezed next to me in the bike lane.

"I remember you."

"Oh, you remember me?" he said, laughing and smiling.

"Yes, you were the one that wasn't happy with the services offered," I said.

"Oh, so you *do* remember me."

"I had to add you to the 'no' list," I told him. No blow would diminish his pride.

"Really?" he said, laughing with a mirthful smile. "So how's business? Have you finally expanded your services?" he asked with a wink.

"No, I don't do that, just like I told you before. I don't need to. Business is great. I rented a studio."

"So you never work out of your home?" he asked.

"No."

"That's probably a good idea," he said.

"So, what have you been doing for body rubs?" I asked. I couldn't remember if Griffin had ever tried to book with me again, but I knew it had been a couple seasons since I had last seen him.

"I found someone in Denver. And she did *everything*. Deep-French kissing even. I didn't even have to ask."

I wanted to ask if "everything" included anal, but that seemed an odd thing to ask in a raised voice over the din of passing cars and other bikers.

I asked if this supposed "everything" girl advertised as a body rub girl or escort. Escort, he said. At a mere $200. I suggested he keep her number.

"She even gave me her *real* name and her *real* phone number," he bragged, as he leaned closer to me, still pedaling furiously to keep up. At this point, I was making the turn onto my street, and knew that although Griffin lived near me, he certainly didn't live on my street.

"If you don't mind," he said, as he followed me to continue retelling his sexual escapades with the woman who'd given him her real name and number. "And she was your age," he said. I assumed he meant the fake age I gave everyone: 31.

This was not a guy who would have had a hard time getting laid, in my opinion. Attractive, gainfully employed, a speedy bike rider. No problems—that is, until he opened his mouth and revealed his emotional quotient.

Griffin volunteered that when he'd tried to book again with the do-everything escort, out of a hotel on such-and-such street off a busy interstate in a sketchy section of Denver, she was a no-show. At this point, I reached my house and Griffin had the sense to make a U-turn.

Most men appear to understand the difference between a body rub girl and escort. To patronize the former with expectations of the latter is a bad play. It's a shame Griffin didn't understand this difference before he'd booked with me. And *psst* . . . likely *not* her "real" name or number. Or her real age. He'd be wise not to believe a word that comes out of our mouths.

33

WHY I DIDN'T DO OUTCALL

"Do you have any pets?" I asked Joe as I rubbed his back. Joe was a regular, but he was a client I only agreed to see after I leased a studio because something about him seemed odd on the phone.

When I saw him for the first time, I was pleasantly surprised: late forties, friendly, quirky, slightly resembling George Clooney with a few extra pounds. Turned out Joe also had great taste in music and was a cat lover.

Joe came to see me weekly. He was single and didn't seem to get much female intimacy. Like some of the other singles, with a little makeover, Joe would've had women lined up. A good starting point would have been his underwear, as in, wearing it. In all my days watching men undress, I was amazed how many guys went commando during the warmer months. Skipping the undergarments is a big fashion and hygiene faux pas. The penis really deserves two fabric barriers (at least!).

In our session, Joe mentioned a cat he had that had developed diabetes. He administered insulin for many months and then she deteriorated. He laid next to her, gazed in her eyes for her last breath, and she passed—his words, not mine. It was winter; the ground was hard and Joe put the cat in the freezer.

"In the freezer? Like a freezer attached to the fridge?" I asked.

I imagined, perhaps, a separate freezer, one in the garage, one that could be left on and forgotten until the ground softened and kitty could be laid to rest.

"The freezer in my apartment."

"Is it a really big freezer? How did you have space?" Logistically, this was hard to imagine. Among all the veggie burgers, nuggets, and frozen berries, I'd have no room for a cat. Never mind the appetite sabotage.

"I don't keep anything in my freezer," Joe said. "You probably think I'm weird."

"No, of course not," I said. "But didn't you worry that someone else would come over and open the freezer?" I mean really, what a way to turn off a woman. She reaches for some ice and ends up with a tail?

"No one comes over to my apartment," he said. "You probably think I'm weird. My sister thinks I'm crazy."

"No, not at all. Time to flip over."

This was exactly why I didn't do outcall. You just don't know what kind of carcasses people are hiding in their apartments.

34

THE SUMMER DOLDRUMS

When I started the body rub business I had trouble keeping up with my phone calls. My phone was off while I was in a session, and then when I finished for the day, I was never in the mood to return calls to let them know I was not taking any more appointments. *And why should I bother? There's more than enough business.*

That flurry of business, I learned, had two causes: 1) being sparkly and new, and 2) brisker weather that drove men indoors toward the naked, hairless bodies of women. I was no longer new and I suspected clients were spending more time basking in the sun and playing golf.

The first time I noticed my business taking a dip, I was convinced my phone wasn't working. I called my body-rub phone from my home phone and determined it was, in fact, working and was immediately seized with fear that I was already a has-been. And then I started getting reviews. The first one was unsolicited, and seeing the spike in business from one review, I began to solicit additional reviews from content regulars. With favorable reviews, my phone once again rang more than I could handle.

New clients came to me and acknowledged it was because of the reviews. These clients were the type who visited Backpage frequently, thought about making the call, but never did out of concern that I was either with law enforcement or a scammer. Reviews removed those fears, but I suspected that this new fleet of clientele would diminish, because most men will only patronize a body-rub girl a few times a year.

As a preemptive strike, I began advertising, "Foot lovers welcome," to stave off another slump. I also included an advertisement under the Fetish section. The majority of responses were too odd for me to accommodate, but I did get enough new clients from the foot advertisements that it was a successful strategy.

After the podophiliacs and paranoid clients had made their way through my studio turnstiles, I tried to find a way to deal with the summer doldrums. I first noticed it a couple of days before the Fourth of July weekend. I was getting just a couple calls a day, if that. Barbecues, boats, and golf were the body-rub girl's enemy!

During these slow periods, I felt the need to take any appointment: any person and anytime. As they say, it's not a good idea to go shopping when you are hungry. During this slow time, I once took a 10:30 p.m. appointment at the studio.

The late-night guy turned out to be an attractive and polite twenty-something who texted me the next day: "Somehow you released all the negativity from my body!" Going to the studio at such a late hour filled me with trepidation. I desperately wanted my phone to ring as frequently as it once had so that I could nix the evening appointments. I felt a particular urgency because I was going on vacation the following week and wanted to squeeze in extra hours. The extra appointments never came, but I planned on using the vacation to brainstorm.

35

Out at Sea

In mid-July, I visited my family on the East Coast. I stayed with my sister, sharing a room with her extreme-couponing cache, where every drawer, closet, cranny and nook was crammed with dozens of "free" tubes of toothpaste, contact solution, Zantac, tampons, and mouthwash.

Alex and I finally split for good just before I left on my vacation. We'd broken up before, but this time it felt solid, like the final felling of a beetle-infested elm. I agreed with one of the commenters on my blog who stated that Alex was likely not okay with what I did. His sentiments were echoed by a couple of regulars I had confided in.

Alex made no mention of my profession when we had our last conversation. He claimed he could not afford a girlfriend. This justification seemed odd to me given that he was the kind of boyfriend who split the bill when he'd ordered more than his share and got out the calculator when he'd had less. He claimed that when he was spending time with me, he wasn't able to work, and this translated to money lost. It felt like a cheap shot. Did he really calculate how much money he could've been making repairing drywall while he was doing me doggy?

As one of my regulars said, given the state of his finances—broke—he really couldn't afford *not* to have a girlfriend.

I was relieved. I didn't blame him for wanting me to quit body rubs, but I wasn't ready to do it. The dilemma held us in relational limbo, and I felt unfair for getting topless with men each day and then expecting Alex to be my monogamous boyfriend. If I dated again, I'd be keeping my business to myself.

With Alex in the back of my mind, I planned a trip to the beach with my family. On my suggestion, we booked a whale/dolphin-watching boat trip with my parents, sister, brother-in-law, and their three small children in Cape May, New Jersey.

I had been on sea vessels before. I had traversed the equator with the help of Dramamine. But the placid Atlantic? Just a couple of hours in the ocean? Nah.

In the bay, waters were calm and we strolled about the ship with our rented binoculars, poking at a lonely horseshoe crab in a metal tub, enjoying the sun and breeze, and scarfing down complimentary sugary sweet snacks and juice. Once we entered the ocean, the waves rocked the boat so much it was impossible to move about without holding on to something. A recent storm had created greater-than-average turbulence.

My nephew was the first to turn green. He didn't say a word, just stared down at his shoes and sat. Then I began to feel miserable. My mother, sitting next to me, complained that a sea gull had just pooped on her foot. A pinkish dollop of vomit had appeared between her toes from above. And then another, much larger dollop hit the deck, causing the passengers to scatter and ruining a perfectly good seat. I looked above and saw an ill child hanging over the railing. "That's not a seagull," I said. "That's complimentary Tastykakes." One by one, children and adults slumped into seating, and intermittently tossed their heads over the rail.

One of the whistling crew members stopped by our seats on the side of the boat, which is the best location to reduce motion sickness. Sitting within the confines of the boat made it worse.

"That's not a happy face," the crew member said as he looked at my nephew. "The best thing to do is to look out at the horizon. And, if you have the need, feel free to paint the canvas," he said, swiping his palm in the direction of the sea. Still whistling, he then grabbed a bucket filled with greenish blue liquid and used a long-handled mop to clean the rail, deck, seat, and my mother's toes, still whistling.

Once we re-entered the bay, the waves and motion sickness subsided and the kids were up and about once again. Just before docking, an announcement came on reminding us of how hard the crew worked for us and that a gratuity was always appreciated, and was, in fact, the greatest portion of the crew's compensation.

This whistling man had cleaned vomit from my mother's toes and gave me a critical piece of advice—look at the horizon—how could I not tip? As I exited the boat, Whistling Man stood at the top of the exit ramp with a wide grin, holding a small bucket labeled "tips." I stuffed his bucket with money and watched as others, mostly the vomiters, tossed in fives and tens. A man in front of me with two young children who were the sickest sheepishly put a generous tip in the bucket. I've seen that chagrined expression on my clients' faces before. And I know it often makes for a good tip.

36

Ms. Nosypants

My first day back from vacation, I worked a full Saturday at the studio. Usually, on the weekends, the other masseuses and Ms. Bossypants were not around.

Given that, I always tossed all of Ms. Bossypants gross slippers and obnoxious signs in the closet, turned up the music, and went about my business. When I came back from my lunch break, there sat a pair of frumpy Birkenstocks in the place where Ms. Bossypants demanded that people remove their shoes. Was someone actually doing business? Seriously, I never understood how these ladies made their share of the studio rent.

I peered down the hall and heard the sounds of massage music— the kind a *real* masseuse plays. I had hoped that the beginnings and endings of our sessions would overlap, providing no opportunity for chitchat.

I made the mistake of keeping my door open just a crack while waiting for my next appointment. Someone knocked. *Seriously? Who knocks on a massage door?*

"Hi, I'm Janice," she said, after I opened the door an additional two inches. I introduced myself, giving my real name, since that's the name Maura knew. I contemplated telling these women my fake name, but it was too likely that we would cross paths while in the company of my friends. The thought of explaining *that* made it seem easier just to provide my real name.

After our brief interchange, where Janice explained that she had to move my purse because it was in the way of her sheets, I went back to waiting for my client. I could hear Janice puttering about the suite. And, if you can believe this, she found the slippers and lined them up neatly back where they'd been. Was Ms. Bossypants a hypnotist as well as physical therapist?

We had a small waiting room at the center of the suites. Usually when a client came through the door, loud chimes jangled and I grabbed the person before they had a chance to sit down or say anything.

Where the hell was my client? He was ten minutes late, which was pretty unusual. Most guys were extremely punctual when it came to getting a rub. No one wanted their tardiness to shorten their massage time. I had seen this client before so I knew he wasn't going to be a no-show.

Then I heard Janice's voice outside the below-grade easement window in my studio: "Gee, I don't know. I don't think there's a Melissa here." My client! I pushed back the curtains to look, and the two were scratching their heads and pointing at other offices in the courtyard.

I opened my studio door, sprinted through the waiting area, up the steps to the courtyard and waved to my client, "Hey, Tim."

"I thought you said your name was Anna," Janice screwed her face up as if she had tasted something sour.

"Oh, he just got confused," I said, hoping Tim would keep his mouth zipped. And as we came down the stairs to the waiting room, Tim managed to practically knock himself unconscious by hitting his head on the ascending staircase.

"I've never seen someone do that before!" Janice chirped.

Brother.

37

THE FOOT JOB

Once, a client showed up at my studio door with an erection. After stepping inside, he proclaimed that he was very excited for our session as he pushed his member down, through his khakis, making it spring back like a jack-in-the-box. It was a first for me, and I took it as an opportunity to engage in the Happy Beginning: starting off a session with a hand job—or in this client's case—a foot job.

He was a self-proclaimed podophiliac. Apparently "the wife" did not enjoy foot jobs and only begrudgingly acquiesced. And that is where I came in.

The client laid down on the massage table, face up, while I also laid down on the table in the opposite direction. I squirted lotion on the bottoms of my feet and rubbed his cock up and down with my feet. The foot job certainly rivals abdominal crunches in terms of a core workout.

"You're amazing," he breathed, blowing out hard with bulging eyes as he sat up to watch my feet.

"A shame your wife doesn't like to do this," I said.

"Yeah, do you?"

"I love it." It's a big turn-on for a guy when they think I'm into it. I needed him to hurry because my ab muscles were burning.

With head thrown back, my client came and then his entire body went limp on the table. Most Happy Beginners also opt for a Happy Ending.

"Want to roll over and I'll massage your back?" I asked.

"I should get back to work," he said.

"Really?" He had only used up fifteen minutes of an already-paid-for one-hour session.

"I've already gotten more than my money's worth," he said.

I had been perfecting my foot job since expanding my Backpage ad to "Foot lovers welcome." Foot-loving maneuvers didn't stop at foot jobs, though. Many respondents liked to suck my toes, put my feet on their stomach, face, or crotch. While some licked, others sniffed. And though it struck me as odd, it felt like one of the more harmless things I offered.

A happy beginning and happy ending was also referred to as "multiple shots on goal" or MSOG. A repulsive term, in my opinion, where sex is likened to a game: one where the male is the aggressor and the female is defending herself. Not all MSOGers were young and spry. I charged more for the dual-happiness body rub, usually $150 per hour, and reserved the extra funds for my future carpal tunnel treatment.

38

THE BUTT KISSER

Periodically I ran a $100-per-hour special to bump up business. I do this if I am heading out of town for awhile, am in a body rub marathon mood, or am in urgent need of cash.

Butt Kisser (BK) responded to my special and booked a one hour session. He sounded a tad awkward on the phone. I have misjudged people in the past, but generally awkward on the phone shows up as some version of a rotund, bespectacled engineer with unclipped toe nails.

Generally I don't care what a person looks like in a body rub, but a heavily forested ass makes me want to bathe in hand sanitizer after the session.

BK was full of directions: rub here, more pressure, softer, counterclockwise, more attention to the balls and on and on. I don't mind a self-choreographed session as long as he says please, which he did. He ruined it somewhat with adding sweetheart every time.

BK was also full of compliments. "You have beautiful breasts. You have a perfect ass. What do you do to stay in shape?"

"Yoga."

Usually I wear panties with full ass coverage. I know some parlors that offer a thong option, but I don't. In BK's session I happened to be wearing a thong because all my full-coverage panties were in the wash. I let BK touch my ass cheeks a bit. When he got too grabby I scooted out of range and gave him a look, prompting an immediate, "Sorry, sweetheart," whistled through a space between his two front teeth.

After the apology, he quieted down, then, "Can I kiss you?" I stopped touching him. "Just kidding, that's a joke because you said no kissing on your ad."

It wasn't a joke. There is a Brazilian saying: Throw out a green fruit and hope to get back a ripe one.

"I don't kiss, sorry."

"That's a shame," he said.

Not really.

"Your ass is so perfect, can I kiss it?" he asked, rising up on his elbows, red-faced and sweaty even though the AC was on high.

"No."

"What if I give you another twenty dollars?"

"No, sorry," I said, resuming his body rub.

"I can give you forty."

I shook my head. He only had 15 minutes left.

"How about a hundred? Just a kiss."

"Just a kiss?" I asked.

"Yes," as he practically leapt off the table and grabbed a hundred out of his Dockers.

"I'm keeping my panties on, though," I looked at the money in his fist.

"No, because I have to slobber down the middle."

No previous mention of the slobber.

"Please, please, I really need to do it. I need to kiss your ass and slobber on you."

"Sorry, no," I said, with just a few minutes left before he was to get his grand finale.

"One last offer, two hundred."

That's $300 for a one-hour session. Usually that amount of money will buy a guy sex with a decent-looking escort.

Tempting, but I declined. The kiss and slobber may have lasted a few minutes, but the memory of a stodgy engineer's tongue between my ass cheeks would've been forever. And the therapy would cost far more than $300.

39

ASIAN MASSAGE PARLORS

In my town, there are about four Asian Massage Parlors (AMPs), and I got the dirt on their operations from my clients. I've always wondered how these businesses get away with what they do—hand jobs, blow jobs, and sex.

An AMP has a certain look–cheap 1980s blinds always drawn, neon OPEN sign, the use of the word "parlor" that tips off most men with a hankering for a rub and tug. Not everyone, however, picks up on the differences between a legitimate massage parlor and an illegal one.

A few months earlier, two male friends and I were having lunch at a Mexican restaurant with an AMP next door and one of them scoffed at the brazenness of the establishment while the other told him he was crazy. The naïve one proclaimed that he had, in fact, gone in and asked for a massage and they mentioned nothing about a hand job(!). The savvy friend rolled his eyes in a gesture of defeat. I was silent, focusing on my guacamole, perhaps letting a half-smile slip. Of course an AMP desk front attendee wouldn't mention a hand job upfront. Usually, they give the price for a massage and once the guy is in the room, they offer the hand job or "other service" at an extra price.

This particular AMP also advertised acupressure (not to be confused with acupuncture), which is a code word for release. White, vinyl, eighties-style blinds were always drawn in the front waiting room and this business's idea of signage included peel-and-stick letters on the front door: BEST BODY THERAPY IN TOWN!. Let's be real, the front window doesn't exactly conjure up feelings of a spa experience, because an AMP doesn't need to create a spa ambience when they are serving up hand jobs. In addition, hours of operation that include late nights (hence the neon signs) and weekends are a good tip-off.

In an AMP, the massage rooms usually resemble seedy bedrooms and the masseuse speaks little or no English. At the most popular AMP in town, they charge $60 for a massage and require a $60 tip for a happy ending. One seasoned AMP patron told me that these prices are usually negotiable. If that's true, then only one of my clients is aware of that because the rest have paid whatever the asking price is. I've also heard from my clientele that a massage and blow job is a $60 fee and $100 tip, which can be bartered down to a $80 tip, but then the woman will short you on the massage by fifteen minutes.

The three biggest complaints I hear about these places, besides the fear of being more easily caught because of a police raid, are the advanced age and homeliness of the women (at this particular place, anyway), the language barrier, and concerns about contributing to human trafficking.

If for no other reason than the human the human trafficking component, I strongly advise against going to AMPs or any other jack shack set up *entirely* with women who only speak broken English, particularly Ukrainians. It's impossible to know if your provider is there by free will, and likely many are not, having been duped by a trafficker. A U.S. State Department Report, one of the most comprehensive on trafficking, claims nearly 800,000 women are trafficked worldwide, many of them ending up in brothels and massage parlors.

According to humantrafficking.org, these women are generally persuaded to come to the United States with promises of modeling jobs or college scholarships. Once they get here, they are treated as slaves who have to work off their "debt" and in some cases, are forced to live in the parlor where they are beaten and raped. Perhaps there are some Asian women who work there of their own volition, but how can you really know? And besides, if more Asian women were doing it freely, then I believe I'd see more former AMP workers going independent.

While taking a photo of my local AMP for a blog post on AMPs, I noticed a middle-aged, white guy with a bad comb-over who had presumably parked in the next lot over and was walking nervously in my direction. He was looking at my camera and I could practically smell the perspiration. Clearly he was a paranoid patron. After the fifth bobble head-turn in my direction, I put a quick end to his staring by turning the camera in his direction and pretending to snap a picture of him. I have never seen a pudgy man in tasseled loafers dart so fast in my life. Perhaps I generated a new client.

40

A SUGAR DADDY OFFER

Martin had a weekly 1.5-hour appointment that included a happy beginning and happy ending. Occasionally, he would book another, shorter appointment within the same week if he happened to be in the neighborhood. In short, his patronage paid my monthly utilities, groceries, and then some. Given Martin's job (pre-retirement), car, house, and lifestyle, his extracurricular activity didn't appear to be a financial burden.

Martin was one of my favorites. He was intelligent, vibrant, and full of self-control, yet he was a self-proclaimed former sex addict. He was also a smoker and therefore looked well older than his 60-something years.

As a recovering sex addict, Martin was well-versed in the escort world and regaled me with stories. He claimed I was naïve. And I think he found that endearing. He had also pleaded with me not to go any further in the industry, claiming he had seen it shatter lives.

During one of our sessions, I mentioned a website, www.seeking-arrangement.com, which had been getting a lot of media attention.

This website was a sugar daddy/sugar baby version of match.com, where the sugar daddy offered a stipend to baby in exchange for dates (i.e., sex).

Given Martin's opinions about escorting ruining lives, I expected him to be equally opposed to such a scenario. Instead, he told me about a couple he knew who had such an arrangement. The sugar baby was a beautiful and single forty-something woman who had aspirations of starting her own business. She had also worked as an escort. Sugar daddy was a wealthy sixty-something father, married to a frigid woman; the kids and wealth made divorce tricky. For a considerable sum, sugar daddy was entitled to two dinner dates per week, whereby one date was just dinner and the second included "play time." Apparently, daddy had erectile dysfunction, so play time did not include penetration, just use of toys, thus the term "play time." In addition, sugar daddy cosigned baby's business loan. Other rules included no escorting for baby, although dating others was okay; just no sex for hire. It was alleged that daddy was in love with baby, but not vice versa.

"It's really worked out quite well for them," Martin told me as I hugged him goodbye.

Later that night, while I was drinking a margarita on the patio of a Mexican restaurant with a potential Boy Friday, my phone kept vibrating. While potential Boy Friday went to the bathroom, I quickly read Martin's texts offering a "mutually beneficial" relationship. "As in sex?" I texted.

"Yes, that's usually the point. Were you worried that it would or wouldn't include sex?" he replied.

At that point in my life, I didn't think it was possible to be attracted to a man in his sixties. In addition, Martin must have lost a lot of weight at one point and unfortunately it left him with skin that sagged so badly that his stomach slipped down past his penis when he stood, reminding me of a melting popsicle. He also had hammer toes, nail fungus, and varicose veins. I loved Martin for his insides and patronage, not the covering.

Potential Boy Friday was back and I slipped the phone in my pocket while it vibrated another dozen times. I would learn later that

Martin was listing the pros of such an arrangement: no jealousy, financial freedom, the ability to cut back, but not stop, my body rub business, his maturity and sensibility. And, most interestingly, he suggested that he had tips for overcoming my lack of physical attraction to him. (Though curious, I never found out what these tips were.)

A couple margaritas and the thought of having sex with a man my father's age was making potential Boy Friday look awfully appealing. Once he paid, we left for another venue before going back to my place.

I later politely declined Martin's offer, telling him that if I were to choose anyone to be my sugar daddy, it would be him, but I just couldn't cross that line. I still liked my sex to be free. He said he understood and scheduled our next regular session. His desire for more than a weekly body rub, however, continued to be a problem.

SUMMER

41

I Changed My Identity

August was not the best month for the body rub business—the end of summer left me jumping every time the phone rang. I was still getting about fifteen appointments per week, but I felt like I had to *work* for it. Body rubs were an impulse buy, so I found myself always needing to be within thirty minutes of my studio—asking clients to wait a couple hours was often the loss of a customer.

I blamed my slump on the summer doldrums. Men were on vacation, getting kids back to school, and soaking up the last bits of long days and warm weather. And woeful economic indicators made me wonder finally if $120 body rubs were too expensive.

I would've dropped my price permanently to boost business, but I hated to lower it to $100 if they were willing to pay $120. I figured some market research would determine the proper price point. I placed two ads, one offering $100 for Melissa, a known entity with mostly fantastic reviews, and the other offering $120 for a new girl, Abigail. I also altered the tone of the Abigail ad. Melissa advertised as smart and straightforward, highlighting her studio location and good reviews, whereas Abigail, the new girl, was flirtier. So as not to give Abigail all the advantages of sexiness, the picture I included was only of my eyeball, and Abigail was a year older than Melissa.

Sensual and Amazing Abigail
I got into this business because I love Men! Our time together will be unforgettable!!! I have a soothing touch and a compassionate demeanor.
I'm slender, tiny, and toned.
Call 970-555-1RUB for an appt. Sorry, but I don't answer blocked calls or texts.
Not an escort service. No switching.
Poster's age: 32

Melissa's ad incorporated the identity I had been using from the beginning, including a standard full-body and in-lingerie (no-face) photo:

Sensual Body Rub by Melissa
I'm sweet, passionate and discreet! Taking day and evening appts. $100 special for an hour-long session. I'm the only independent with a clean and professional studio setting and fantastic reviews on the local review board!
*Not an escort. No kissing, switching, or cuddling. Call **970-555-1515**.*

Abigail's ad did not disclose an hourly rate. Most Backpage ads for body rubs didn't include a price. I can only assume this was a strategy meant to hook a guy once the provider got him on the phone. I had always included my prices in my Melissa ads, in the spirit of efficiency. Only once did I forget and I spent the day answering, "How much do you charge?" more than a dozens times in a few hours. But in my Abigail ad, I chose not to include the price because it was another way for me to gauge a price point by how often the guy booked after hearing the price, particularly with Melissa's posted price at only $100 per hour. Would my phone ring for Abigail only to ring a minute later for Melissa in search of the cheapest rub?

Rather than buy a new pre-paid cell phone, I created a new number through Google Voice, one with the word RUB in it. (I later had a client tell me the number with RUB in it was off-putting because it seemed too professional.)

I wished I had discovered Google Voice before I bought my pre-paid cell. Google Voice enabled me to create a phone number and then have that number sent to the Melissa prepaid phone so that when a guy called, it would show up in my list of contacts if they had patronized Melissa. This protocol assumed I kept an updated contact list.

The ad produced a barrage of phone calls for Abigail, reminding me of the good ole days of picking and choosing clients based on how sexy a guy's voice sounded. A couple of my regulars called to make appointments with Melissa, but I was getting virtually no new calls for my $100 special.

Men were giddy and curious when they called Abigail, one even exclaiming how gorgeous my picture was. Of my eyeball? As was the case early on with the Melissa ads, many guys just liked to call and talk to a body-rub girl, and consider scheduling, but never followed through.

For every ten calls that Abigail got, Melissa got one. Seriously, ten to one and Abigail had *no* reviews. Poor Melissa, all washed up at the age of 31 and only six months in the business.

I could have understood the results if Melissa was the tiny bru-nette and Abigail was a statuesque blonde, but no, there was no advertised difference in appearance.

The first person I booked as Abigail was Mike. He didn't come up in my phone so I assumed he was new. I gave him the address of my studio and told him I'd wait for him in the reception room.

Peering from the reception area window, I watched as a mor-bidly obese man slumped out of a truck and walked up the path. I realized this was an old client—a previous client of Melissa's! I didn't know who he was because it had been more than four months since he had last seen me, so he'd been deleted from my phone contacts. And he did not connect Abigail to Melissa because when he last saw me I worked at another location. The address I gave was new to him.

During our first encounter I believed he'd had a truly great experience. We had talked, I had rubbed, and he had come. He had tipped me and mentioned that next time he booked an appointment, he'd bring some photos of his arrowhead collection. It had seemed genuine.

Would he turn and go away once he discovered I wasn't a new girl? I opened the door, smiled, and said, "Hi Mike, how have you been?"

His face didn't falter and he didn't ask why I'd changed my name. He just smiled and followed me upstairs. He knew and I knew. Once we got down to business we resumed old topics of conversation: the $35,000 sale of his best arrowhead, his thyroid condition, and a few bits about me that he remembered.

The session went well and once again he seemed pleased, although he didn't mention this time that he'd be back.

I felt oddly betrayed, or at least a little stumped. After he left, I paced the studio and tried to think of why he would seem to enjoy a session and only wait until a new girl popped up in town to book again. It wasn't a factor of money; that much I knew for sure.

Could it be that he was embarrassed? Or was he afraid that someone might not want to book with him a second time after they'd seen that he was 200 pounds overweight?

There are some unpleasant things that happen to the human body when someone carries that much extra weight. Sores develop in the folds of fat. In addition, the folds don't get a lot of air and thus don't exactly smell like a Rocky Mountain meadow. This scenario is particularly rough when a guy comes directly from a long summer day of hard labor.

The other problem is that a guy of Mike's size can't see his penis, no matter how much twisting and craning he does. While I was jerking off Mike and as the minutes ticked, he attempted to peer over his belly to check the status of his member. "Is it still hard?" he asked, breathing heavily and sweating.

"Yes," I said, with my arm about to fall off from trying so hard. He did eventually come. And once he had cleaned up and got his clothes back on, he handed me a ten and asked if I would tie his shoes. We hugged goodbye. No matter what a client looked like—and I've seen it all, from sores (the non-contagious, non-genital variety) and oozing back acne, to you name it—I have never said a negative word about a client's naked body. And I generally tried to find a nice thing to say because everybody has something appealing about them.

Mike was not alone in his preferences for the new girl. One by one, I watched the parade of old clients book with Abigail. They showed up, pretended like I was just an old friend. No one mentioned that it had been months since they last booked. Yet they'd called Abigail within twenty-four hours of the ad posting.

My limited research proved that fresh meat trumped good reviews and a better price. I never received back-to-back calls for Abigail then Melissa from a guy in search of the cheapest price. I found no difference between offering $100 versus $120. The good news was that my research put an end to the $100 special.

42

I Rented Another Studio

Although I loved the studio I shared with Maura, I needed another studio with more hours of availability. I also felt it was best to keep moving, particularly with the likes of Janice (aka Ms. Nosypants) and Jen (aka Ms. Bossypants) nosing around. And Maura still hadn't given up on the idea of being my friend and trading massages. If she ever got suspicious enough to install a nanny cam, it would've been a traumatizing event for her.

The new place was still shared with another health practitioner, Gwendolyn, but she was only there intermittently on weekends. The new studio was a solitary room on the third floor with windows overlooking trees, giving it a tree house feel. And as luck would have it, a flood had wiped out the first floor, making for a fully renovated waiting room and bathroom. In addition, rent included common area maintenance, thus preventing all the squabbling that went on in my current suite about whose turn it was to empty the trash.

43

No Need to Try Too Hard

A bigail was a hit and a boost to my income stream. As I massaged old clients who reappeared as a result of my new identity, I detected a pattern. Some of the most reliable clients did not return after they failed to perform.

One client, Ron, had been a faithful, once-a-week, married client whose sessions were filled with moans and groans of delight and compliments about my touch, my ass, and my perky breasts. He called my sessions "a slice of heaven."

During one session, Ron was not able to come. Sometimes, it just didn't happen. I even gave Ron an extra fifteen minutes in the spirit of keeping him happy. I practically gave myself tendonitis.

When Ron also realized he wasn't going to come, he sat up, looked at the clock, and said, "Wow, I'm taking up too much of your time. I've got to go," and with that he dressed and shot out the door without even washing his hands. From time to time, I'd wonder what happened to Ron. Perhaps he went away for the summer, or was being more faithful to his wife, or working extreme hours.

Yet as soon as Abigail appeared, Ron called to book immediately. Ron's inability to come and the cessation of his business were coincidental. Was there a sense of embarrassment?

I certainly held no judgments. It's not like I was having sex with them. I had cranked an extra fifteen minutes into Ron at no extra charge (and with no tip), only for him to stop returning.

When Ron came back to Abigail, he didn't say why he suddenly stopped coming, but he resumed all his praise, moans, and groans.

From that point on, when a guy couldn't come within a reasonable timeframe, I didn't give myself tennis elbow. In most cases, if they didn't come, they didn't come back.

And, if things got slow, I could always switch up my name and location again. And they'd come back, pretend nothing was amiss, perhaps say, "Weren't you Abigail?" yet pay nonetheless. In this business, it's not personal; it's just about the money.

44

GOING BLONDE

The boost in my business from creating the new body-rub girl, Abigail, prompted me to create Tiffany, who was blonde. (Strippers wear wigs all the time, so why not?)

I hoped to entice those men who preferred blondes. The wig also enabled me to craft an ad that included at least one photo with a partial shot of my face, which was something that Max, the owner of Mile High Escorts, had told me brought more business.

I went downtown to a costume store and bought a blonde wig with copper highlights for a mere $30 (tax deduction!). When I tried it on for my current Boy Friday, his eyes brightened. "It looks like real hair," he said.

I told him I was preparing for a local festival in September where revelers don outrageous costumes, ride their bikes, and get sloppy drunk on beer.

Once again I created another number through Google Voice. At the back of my mind, I worried that a current customer would book with Tiffany and be pissed when he realized I was just Melissa with a wig. I was pushing it by wearing a wig. It was a chance I was willing to take. If the guy seemed miffed, I hoped to joke it off. I had learned with the Abigail ad that even when the guy realized I wasn't a new girl, with money in hand and boner in pants, they never walked away.

It was getting more difficult to keep all the names straight. When I booked an appointment, I wrote down his name and my name, as well, so I knew how to introduce myself. Tiffany added the complication of making sure that I had enough time between clients to put my long, brown hair in pigtails, fold them under a wig cap, and then put on the wig. No more walking a client downstairs and out the door, just in case a Tiffany client came early after I had finished up with an Abigail or Melissa client.

The first person who booked with Tiffany was a last-minute, familiar voice. I was working in the sunset hours, something I almost never did, but I was hard pressed for cash.

After booking the appointment, I checked the phone number and discovered it was a client whom I had just seen a few days earlier. He was an out-of-town father getting his daughter settled into the local university. I had seen him before in Maura's studio. (I was still renting her studio until she could find a subleasing replacement.)

The out-of-town dad had a new studio address so he had no expectations of a repeat performance. I worried that he might recognize me, throw up his hands and ask what kind of racket I was running. He never did. No one ever did. In fact, the out-of-town dad arrived early, while I was still walking from my car to the front door of the building. We greeted in the dark with no acknowledgment of me as the girl he had seen just a few days earlier.

Similar to my experience with Mike, I was astounded. When he had been out in Colorado visiting a couple months earlier with his daughter, he came to see Melissa, and when he returned, he booked again with Melissa. Then a couple days later, he booked with Tiffany. It shouldn't have been surprising to me because the "hobby" is driven by the desire for variety, but in my naivety, I believed that if I gave a client good service, he should want to come back to me exclusively.

He was easy: a gentleman, a fit and sexy silver fox who loved having his nipples fondled. He loved it so much that when my hands were elsewhere, he continued to rub and turn his nipples like they were knobs on a radio and he was searching for just the right reception.

Once inside, he followed me upstairs to the massage room, I asked for the payment, and still, no flash of recognition.

Perhaps he just wanted to play along, I thought. After all, he came across as a fairly astute man. But then again, how many times had I complained that my father or a boyfriend hadn't noticed my new haircut or highlights? Now this lack of observance was working in my favor.

If Hot Dad was indeed playing along then he was surely doing a fabulous job, because he launched into the same stories that Melissa had heard a few days earlier: his daughter, his job, his now empty nest, his trip to the Middle East for work. Talk about déjà vu.

Since I had seen him before, I wasted no time getting to his nipples. My teensy bit of guilt for pulling one over on him made me want to perform at my best.

"That was amazing," he said, after he put on his pants. "My legs feel like Jell-O."

"Glad you liked it."

I opened the door of the massage room to let him out, but I wasn't able to walk him downstairs because I had another client waiting for me. A client who was expecting brunette Melissa.

"You are the best in town," he said, shaking his head. He had not said this previously to Melissa. "The girl in the red dress." He gave me one last look as he walked out.

The next time he came back into town a couple months later, he first called Tiffany to book a weekend appointment. I wasn't working so I didn't return his call. A few hours later, he called Melissa to book, confirming my belief that he believed me to be two different people.

Not everyone was as unobservant. Sam was one of the first clients who booked with me. He booked weekly for a couple months and then stopped coming. He had never been to my new studio.

As soon as the blonde body rub girl ad was placed, he called. I gave him the address and when I met him down in the waiting room, I recognized him immediately as my once-faithful regular. He looked up sheepishly without any indication of knowing me. I told him to follow me upstairs. As he followed behind me, I wondered if I should just confront the issue right away. "So, long time no see?" or, "How's your summer been? Mine's been great since I went blonde."

I'd leave it up to him to say something first. I already had his money; even if he didn't like the wig, he likely wasn't going to walk out.

I went through my spiel of "get undressed and lie face down," then left the room, trying to come up with appropriate answers for why I changed my hair and name.

Sam had always been a fairly easy customer. He generally lay like a sack of potatoes on the table, asking a few questions here and there and coming quickly and easily.

He laid face down and only turned over when I told him.

On this day, I hated to ask him to turn over because I knew he'd have a good look at my face. Even though Hot Dad had seen me within the week, all together he had only seen me twice, both times at night. Sam had gazed at my face quite a few times and always in the bright light of day.

Until he flipped over, I'm convinced Sam didn't have a clue that Blonde Girl was just Melissa with a wig. With just fifteen minutes left, I went to work on his legs and bulging belly. He told me about his boat (again) and how he had packed on the pounds from drinking beer while boating.

Then suddenly he stopped talking and scrunched up his face.

"You know, you look like another girl, an independent just up the road," he said.

"Really?" I said. *Shit, should I just confess now?*

"Hmm, what's her name?" he asked, looking up to the ceiling to help him remember.

"Melissa?" I asked.

"That's it," he said, snapping his fingers. "Do you know her?"

"That's my sister," I said. "We just have different hair." I could have told him I was an alien or had been body-snatched for the summer and he'd probably be okay with it, as long as something was rubbing his cock.

"I knew it," he exclaimed. "I kept thinking you looked familiar. I was going to call her this morning."

"Well, I'm glad you called me instead," I said, lowering my chin and smiling.

"You aren't twins are you?" he asked.

"Yep," I said, turning to smile at him. "We used to work together until we had a falling out." I wrapped one hand around his member and the other around his balls. That usually shut them up right away. Enough of this inquisition.

After his finale, Sam dressed quickly and right before he turned to walk out the door, he paused and said, "I knew you looked familiar. You almost got me," he said, wagging his finger and smiling. Whether he truly believed I was anything other than Melissa's twin, I'll never know.

45

IT'S ALWAYS THEIR FIRST

B eing Tiffany gave me a few insights into the mind of body rub patrons. I learned that some clients liked to claim that this was their first time. Even when it was not. Even when they were seasoned hobbyists.

If a client had seen me only once before and it was more than a month ago, chances were good that I would go unrecognized. I would once again be Sparkly and New Blonde Body-Rub Girl and cash in as a result.

I had several clients who I had seen before (only once) as Melissa that came to see Blonde Body-Rub Girl and emphatically claimed that they were "new to all of this," throwing up their hands with a wobbly smile.

Todd was a mid-forties, stocky man of Hawaiian descent with a badly pitted complexion. I first saw him as Melissa when I was working out of Maura's office, and he mentioned his impending divorce and desire to pursue the escort world. He was a talker and an interesting one, telling me stories of his international work for the government defusing bombs. He also mentioned traveling to overseas brothels. Rather than go full service, he claimed, he settled for the massages, hand jobs, and blow jobs.

"Do you offer any additional services?" he had asked.

"I'm flattered, but no."

Just barely a month later he booked with Blonde Body-Rub Girl. When I greeted him in the waiting room, I immediately recognized him. Surely he'd recognize me. The man defused bombs for a living; you would think he'd have an eye for the meticulous.

"Do I know you?" I asked, smiling. I wanted to get it out of the way if he did.

He instantly looked alarmed. "No, I don't think so." Eyes wide, deer in headlights, like he wanted to bolt out the door. "Do you?" he choked out.

"No, I guess I thought you looked familiar. My mistake," I said. "We'll be upstairs." I turned towards the stairs and gave a quick look behind to make sure he was following me.

After he paid, undressed, and I re-entered the room, he asked, "So, you think you know me?" The poor guy was now paranoid that somehow I knew him, but he couldn't place me, therefore leaving him at risk of stripping his anonymity.

"No, I'm sure I'm wrong."

A couple minutes into the massage, Todd loosened up and began telling me about his bomb job (again). He also told me how this was his very first rub and apologized if he appeared nervous.

"Your first, huh?" I said.

"Yep. I'm totally green at this."

This time Todd didn't mention the overseas brothels. Again, he asked if I offered additional services. My hair might change on occasion, but never my answer to that question.

It's unclear to me why patrons wanted to appear as being new to rubs. I was in no position to judge and my only concern was how the client treated me, such as understanding the word "no," not whether they were new or seasoned. In fact, I preferred a guy to have had an erotic massage before. They tended to know the drill and were less paranoid. Todd wasn't the only guy to claim it was his first, when in fact I had seen the client before. They should stick to just lying to their significant others.

46

THANKS FOR THE CONTROVERSY

One morning over coffee, I checked my blog to see how many hits I had gotten so far that day.

In the beginning, I was lucky to get fifty hits per day. Then my little blog grew through mentions in other blogs and ranking high enough in SEO that people found it through Internet searches. I was thrilled when I finally got 460 hits in a day.

Then suddenly, I had already passed 500 hits and it wasn't even 9 a.m. yet.

The way my blog is set up, I can see what incoming links are used to land on my site. I had a sinking feeling when I saw it was the local review board. I wanted to keep distance between clients and readers of my blog, but the gap was narrowing as my blog became more popular.

I clicked on the incoming link's post on the local review board:

And Yes, She's Proud of Scamming
I was bored and googling, when I found this website run by a local massage girl http://secretsofawebcamgirl.com She mentions the review

board a few times (she's reviewed) but what I completely dislike about the vibe of the website is she's basically bragging about new personas to attract clients. Via wigs, new Google voice numbers, different names, etc. Ok, I'm fine with the Backpage roulette wheel, but please, don't be a scammer and blog about it. Sheesh.

Other members of the review board quickly joined the thread, resulting in more than a couple dozen responses, most of them ranting about my use of wigs (strippers do it) and changing my identity (the first one I created wasn't the real me, anyway) and calling out clients (of course all names and identifying details are changed), and claiming my behavior was typical of a drug addict.

A couple commenters acknowledged that my writing was good, perhaps too good to be an addict, and others claimed, "too good to be true."

My blog reached more than 2,100 hits that day and overall maintained a higher viewership even after the thread died out. Some members of the review board subscribed and left comments indicating they liked my blog, one person calling it a "gem." I also received some hate e-mail, one person calling me a "faggot and a creep."

Because of the proximity of the haters (Colorado residents), I became quite nervous that someone would retaliate. The first couple of nights after it happened, I slept elsewhere. For a few weeks after the incident, I worried that someone might go so far as to screw with me by booking phony appointments, yelling at me on the phone, or displaying some other form of aggression at an actual appointment. No one ever did. It's one thing to rant and rave behind a computer, but luckily no one got riled up enough to confront me physically or verbally.

The comments, however, struck me as amazing. The posters were a mix of escorts and the guys who patronized them, known as "hobbyists." What we all do is illegal, and most hobbyists, as well as body rub patrons, are married. I would've thought this group would be the last to judge; I certainly knew I wasn't in a position to do so. Amazingly, within the world of infidelity and prostitution, these people have concocted a "code of ethics." Up-selling by an escort was frowned upon; clock-watching was intolerable. If there were any expectations of hobbyists other than paying, I was not aware of it.

I wanted no part of their world, their code of conduct, because to subscribe to such meant I was sinking into it, making it a profession. I just wanted to put on my wig, get my money, and be gone.

47

MILE HIGH ESCORTS' TRAIL OF TEARS

While I was browsing the local review board, I looked up Mile High Escorts—the place I interviewed with before I decided to be independent. I came across a review of one of Mile High's escorts, Cassandra, who was tagged as a "rip off."

I was quoted one price on the phone by the agency, but when Cassandra showed up, she called the agency, got off the phone and told me the price had gone up $25 because she had to travel to me (my location was obviously known when I had booked with the agency originally). Not wanting to cause problems with the agency, which I hoped to use again, I forked over another $25 and settled in for some fun. Cassandra began to strip. I immediately noticed her MANY stretch marks (this is why her pics never show her midriff). It's sort of a personal turn-off, but I go with it. I touched her breasts and immediately noticed they are augmented and as hard as rocks—really a terrible boob job. Upon commenting on them, Cassandra responded that at a certain age, a woman needs a boob

job. Yeah, that and the fact that she has obviously had numerous child-
ren! I ask her how old she really is (she advertised for 26). She responded
40. This is getting to be too much. Then she informs me there will be
no sex, no oral, no French kissing, and I can only touch her tits. Being
horny, I just wanted to get off, so she informed me I could perform self-
service, while looking at her naked, stretch-marked, poorly altered body.
I told her I did not have to pay $200 to service myself. She responded that
I had already paid $200, so I might as well do something because I was
not getting my money back. I decided to try offering her more money and
she offered additional limited service for more than twice the original
price paid. I sent her home.

The company was clearly not concerned about customer satisfaction and expected the girl to deal with the no-sex disappointment.
Max had claimed Mile High was a multi-million dollar cash cow.
Only in the sex industry could a bait-and-switch be so lucrative. Mile
High clearly capitalized off one-timing their customers. There were a
few other Mile High reviews on the board and all were rated as rip-
offs. Mile High might not have been violating any prostitution laws,
but they were unscrupulous.

48

WHAT ARE MY CHANCES OF
GETTING ARRESTED?

M onths into doing rubs, paranoia of arrest crept into my mind.

It is illegal to touch a penis for money. It is illegal to kiss for money. Offering a "body rub" is legal as long as the two previously mentioned acts don't take place and the provider does not call herself a masseuse or a massage therapist. Performing body rubs as a business likely requires a business license, entertainer's license, and "doing business as" (DBA) registration since I used a fake name. Obviously, I hadn't marched into my local and state offices to register.

I believed, perhaps erroneously, that my chances of getting arrested were slim. The out-in-the-open operations of the AMPs were the source of this comfort. Wouldn't the police have gone after them first? At least I wasn't trafficking anyone.

And it wasn't just the AMPs that thrived. While I was still webcam modeling and looking for other work, I responded to an ad for *Boulder Sensations*, a jack shack that hired all ethnicities, with a 60/40 split—60 to the rubber. In our e-mail exchanges, the owner indicated that the establishment was "secure from LE"—LE stood for law enforcement; yes, I had to look it up. How could the owner claim to be free from a potential bust? That was a pretty bold statement. (I decided I'd prefer a 100/0 split and never went further with my inquiries.)

I'd heard that these businesses offered free rubs to police and politicians. I'm just not sure I believed it.

And through my blog, I connected with other body rub girls, some who worked in parlors and others who were independent. One woman wrote:

> *I don't live in Colorado; but I know that where I live, police officers can get naked, have gotten naked, have even received the happy ending and really enjoyed it, and then took the girl to jail afterwards. What a great use of tax dollars! There was a huge report about it in the news, where the officers were having sex with prostitutes and then arresting them. Lots of corruption, but who are they going to believe in court?*
>
> *A friend of mine was arrested because the cop asked, "How much for a blow job?" and she said, "Not for a million dollars." She got charged with solicitation because she was negotiating a sex act for money. They were recording the conversation. The charges were eventually dropped, but she had to go to jail and she spent more than $5,000 in legal fees, and it will always be on her record that she was charged with it, even though she was not found guilty. But, prostitution is a huge problem in my city, there are probably 100 listings on Backpage everyday, and streetwalkers on every corner, so there is a large task force, and lots of tax dollars going into this. And still, they only raid massage parlors approximately twice a year.*
>
> *The truth is, if the cops want to bust you, if you have had complaints from neighbors, or if there is an election going on, then they will find a way to arrest you, no matter what. The police are always right. The least they can charge you with is "massage without a license" and the worst is "prostitution" or "promoting prostitution" and even "criminal syndicate" if you own a business where you employ others.*

With that being said, you are independent, which means you are under the radar. You don't have five girls working under you, which would cause several men coming and going out of your office per hour. Also, you are not in your house in a nice neighborhood with old grannies looking out their window when the men come and go. And the cops honestly don't want to waste their time busting one person when they can go to a big establishment and bust several and the owner and get felony charges. It is more reward for their efforts. Good luck and stay safe! Dee

This woman's interpretation was consistent with what I had read and heard. One of my regulars with a little knowledge of the legal system claimed that even if a guy got naked in preparation for a rub, that didn't necessarily mean he wasn't a cop.

Another reader who lived in Colorado mentioned that in a nearby county, there was a shakedown of a couple massage parlors that offered happy endings when one parlor angled to put the other out of business by snitching to the police. With this information, the police were able to gather enough evidence to charge both establishments. Although I searched, I couldn't find anything relating to this bust, though I believed the blog reader.

Whenever these busts made it to online news sites, the comments from the public, by far, were that there should've been better use of police than busting people paying for hand jobs. One commenter said, "Are we using tax money for a cop to get a hand job?" Jack shacks might be unsavory to the average person, but most online commenters didn't think they were worth taking down.

For whatever it was worth, I took a few measures to lessen my chances of immediate arrest. I never discussed hand jobs or happy endings or any other well-known euphemisms over the phone. Most guys didn't ask such a stupid question, but I got the occasional newbie knucklehead who insisted on getting an answer before he booked. I figured it was better to lose a customer then incriminate myself over a recordable medium. I had the same policy for e-mails and texts.

I also took comfort in changing my identity, phone number, and venue several times. Although I originally switched things up to boost business, it felt better to keep moving and altering.

Before I began a rub, I asked the patron to undress before I stepped out of the room. On only two occasions did the client keep his underwear on. One time was the religious guy. The other guy said he was too uncomfortable to take off his shorts. Neither guy got a release. Although I'd been told otherwise, I figured a police officer wouldn't be allowed to show me his penis as part of a sting or, at least, most officers wouldn't have wanted to—or were prohibited by wifey—to get naked as part of a sting. *How was your day, Honey?*

I tried not to spend a lot of time worrying about this, but I was asked repeatedly by customers how concerned I was, thus making me more fretful. I could tell many of my clients were also worried about being arrested.

Personally, I think rubs should be legal. In other countries, they are. If a guy wants to pay for a release, what business is it of the government's? A hand-job tax could really put a dent in that trillion-dollar deficit! And I can't imagine Clinton hasn't gotten a rub or two in his tenure.

As long as the AMPs and Boulder Sensations are keeping their doors open, I am not exceedingly worried. If they suddenly get busted, I might be off to England, Germany, New Zealand, or Holland.

49

FAKING IT

I had just finished up with a client when I got a call from Joseph, who asked if there was any way I could squeeze him in before the Broncos game in the evening. I told him he could come right away and he quickly got the address, asked if I took credit cards (no, and it was unusual for my clients to even ask) and said he'd be there in twenty minutes. Before he hung up, I made sure to tell him the price was $120 (my ad didn't mention it and he never inquired). He said that was fine and he'd be right over.

I greeted Joseph in my studio's common area and then took him into my studio. Joseph looked to be in his early forties, ruggedly handsome, and smelled like a smoker. He was also missing an arm. Joseph wasn't big on warm smiles, and I couldn't even get him to look me directly in the eye.

As usual, I asked Joseph if we could take care of the payment first. He obliged. Then I told him to take everything off and lie face down on top of the sheets while I briefly stepped out.

When I re-entered the room, Joseph was still wearing his underwear. This concerned me because I feared he was an undercover cop. I never discussed releases over the phone or online but you never knew. I assumed (perhaps incorrectly) that an undercover cop wouldn't bare his penis. Underwear really fucked up my game. In some cases, a guy was just nervous and I gave them a little encouragement to not be shy.

"Would you like to remove everything so that I can massage your buttocks?" I asked.

Joseph lifted his head and said, "Um, no, I'm gonna go with no."

Going to go with no?

My shirt and shorts were already off when I asked the buttocks question, so before I took off my bra, I thought I'd ask first. "Do you want me to be topless?"

"Um, um, your ad said nothing about that," he said. "Wow, how awkward." He cleared his smoker's throat. "No, not awkward," he corrected politely, as if someone had pushed a rewind button on his neck.

I began massaging Joseph's back and looking up directly at me was the inked, soulful face of Christ on the cross, crown of thorns and all. Thank God I hadn't taken my bra off! Had I not stopped to ask Joseph about being topless, I would have been dunking my nipples in Jesus' mouth.

As I massaged Joseph's legs, feet and one arm, each body part revealed more religious tattoos. Joseph's flat stomach had the letters J-E-S-U-S in cursive. One calf had a man of the cloth's palms together in prayer. Another calf tattoo memorialized a grandparent. The wrist displayed the thorns Jesus was forced to wear. No matter where I walked around the massage table, I couldn't help but feel Jesus was watching.

Was it possible that Joseph had thought he was responding to an ad for a legitimate massage? Apparently he did, as he began to describe all his ailments and I had to fake it based on a few YouTube massage videos I'd watched and what I recalled from my own therapeutic sessions. I was simply too uncomfortable to engage him in anything more than limited conversation.

One would think that the price alone would be clue enough. Around here a legitimate massage from a licensed massage therapist generally costs $40 per hour to $70 per hour. Maura had charged $65 per hour with specials occasionally for $45 per hour.

I didn't find Joseph to be overly naïve, as one might expect considering his current situation. He had friends; he mentioned going jet-skiing the day before and meeting buddies at a sports bar later. He seemed like a regular guy, one who really, really loved Jesus, and one who unknowingly responded to the ad of a sex worker.

When the hour was up, I told Joseph that I hope he enjoyed it. I felt a little underdressed in my matching leopard-print lingerie.

"That was great," he said. "I feel so much better."

Oh, *but you could have felt much, much better*, I thought.

50

TAKING IT ABROAD

My first vacation request came from Leo. Leo was a handsome, married guy, one in a touch-starved state. He was a hugger. Although my ad stated, "no cuddling," I'd usually let a naked hug slide occasionally. Sometimes, I just felt badly. If a person was not even getting hugs in a marriage, well then, that's just depressing.

While we were embracing, Leo whispered in my ear that he'd like to take me to Bora Bora (French Polynesia). Leo was a fan of Bora Bora after discovering parasailing. What better place to parasail than above a lagoon of green and blue water, he claimed. His trips had become so frequent that he had bought a small Tahitian-style house overlooking a bay. Now *that* was a turn-on. I loved to travel, but a place like Bora Bora was far out of my financial grasp.

After our session, he followed up with an e-mail reiterating his enjoyment of our time spent and that he really was serious about the trip. Leo was remarkably handsome. He looked to be in his early forties, but after he provided a timeline of his life, I assumed him to be mid-fifties or older. He was tanned and toned. And married. And I didn't really know him that well. A trip could end up being one really, really long bad date.

I mentioned the invite to one of my regulars, one who was well-versed in the escort world, and he promptly mentioned that I should be compensated. This was my business, after all, and nothing was free. He also scoffed at the notion that Leo was simply looking for a traveling buddy.

I responded to Leo's e-mail, saying I was flattered but that my time had to be compensated.

"How much?" he wrote. "How much to take a weekend trip to Denver? Or a motorcycle ride or a week-long vacation to Belize?"

Hmm, I had no idea and I was starting to feel like an escort. He hadn't mentioned sex. But seriously, how could I assume anything else?

Leo claimed in our e-mail exchange that he was just looking for a traveling companion, someone who was smart, cute, and fun. He said his wife was all those things except the last one. He took all his parasailing vacations without her.

After stalling and contemplating it, I decided I just couldn't make the transition from body-rub girl to escort. I told him as much in an e-mail. He let it go. A couple months later he resumed his requests. I couldn't help but think of relaxing under a thatched-roof hut. Yet another temptation of being a body-rub girl.

51

WHEN YOU THINK HE MIGHT BE FALLING FOR YOU

I continued to see Joe weekly and I sensed he was allowing a crush to fester: Joe was the client who kept his dead cat in the freezer until the ground thawed enough to ensure a proper burial.

He was still single—and handsome!

Joe was one of my favorites because he was a talker. The talkers kept me entertained during the boring bits of rubbing. He referred to our sessions as his therapy. A therapy session with a hand job.

I began to suspect a problem during one session in particular. It was THE LOOK. Every woman knows it. I'd rather stick a gloved finger up a client's ass than stare deeply into his eyes. Joe was delivering THE LOOK intently, pleading silently with me to return his gaze. I did. He did not look away. Tick, tock, tick, tock. Still looking.

"Please blink," I said.

"Do I have to?" he asked.

During our session, he said that he had won an award at work, which qualified him for all-expenses-paid Caribbean vacation for two. Did I want to come?

"I can't. I'm dating someone. I have to work," I said

"I'll pay for your week of work."

"You're funny," I said and laughed, feeling his ant-burning gaze on my left cheek.

Shortly after that session, Joe booked again, just a couple days later. He brought music he thought I'd like and asked questions such as, "What do you consider intimacy? Do you believe in fate? What does it take for you to trust someone? Do you think of me as just a client?"

And just before he departed, he pulled out the invitation for the five-star resort from his company. The invitation depicted a swim-up bar, sparkly sand, and an aqua-colored ocean. I hesitantly gave the invitation back to him and told him it looked fun. I made it a point not to repeat rejections.

I think Joe will continue to make offers, look for clues of reci-procated amour, and finding none, will move on to another provider. A shame, I think, because I really do enjoy his company, just not enough to take a week-long vacation with him.

52

SOMEONE KILLED AN ESCORT

Alex called me unexpectedly to tell me that a friend-of-a-neighbor's-friend's-sister was murdered. And she worked as an escort in Denver. "Would you please consider stopping what you do?" he asked. "I'm worried about you." His voice broke a little on the last word.

The story sounded contrived so I asked her name, Googled it, and discovered that yes, she had been found in the back of an SUV after decomposing for quite a few days in a seedy area of Denver.

The story about her death appeared in a Denver newspaper. The part about her being an escort was not included in the article, although they did acknowledge that she had apparently had money problems and a man had secured a restraining order against her. Since the investigation was ongoing, details were sparse about it being a homicide.

Based on what Alex had heard, this woman had a drug problem, which I have heard tends to be more common in the escort world or body rub profession when compared to the general population. Most drug addicts can't hold down real jobs yet need a great income to maintain their habit; escorting and body rubs are often the solution.

"Well, maybe it was her drug use that got her killed," I told Alex. "A lot of escorts have a problem with that."

"I know you think this could never happen to you, but it could," he said.

I don't use illegal drugs, so I suppose that made me feel safer than girls who are willing to take risks to get their fix. I also didn't go to clients' homes or give them my real information.

"In the beginning, you said you wouldn't work late at night. How late did you work last night?"

I had worked late. It wasn't the first time I said I wouldn't ever do something in this business and then did.

"In any case, I'm not an escort," I said. And then I switched the subject, just glad to be speaking to him again.

I would never have told Alex this, but I was always a tad jumpy when I walked from my studio to my car after dark. My mace was always in my hand. Would I have been so concerned if I had just worked a shift as a nurse? Probably not. This was another good reason why coming up with another way to make money was becoming critical.

53

EROTIC MASSAGE 101: SWITCHING

In erotic massage, "switching" is when the masseuse gets massaged by the client. It's also called mutual massage, and it was a popular request among patrons.

When I first started out, I would get the question: "Do you switch?"

When asked over the phone, I said no to switching. During the session, I allowed for a switch only a few times, either because I was attracted to the client or they were a trust-worthy regular with good hygiene.

In the beginning, I received the request for switching so often that I included "No Switching" in my ad for the sake of efficiency. The question went away. After creating Abigail and Tiffany, I neglected to include the "No Switching" to appear more cheery and carefree. The switching requests resumed.

For many guys, being able to give a massage, in addition to fondling breasts, was critical, which was why they asked up front. It's definitely a legitimate question to ask on the phone (i.e., it's not incriminating; but asking if you will get a happy ending over the phone is not a good idea).

Elmer was one of the unfortunate switchers who neglected to ask up front or didn't realize how pivotal it was to the success of his session.

Elmer moaned with delight as I massaged his back and slid my body against his. "That feels amazing," he said. "You're gonna make me want to give you a massage."

I try not to shut a guy down in a session. I don't want him to feel rejected and he wasn't being overly gropey, so I just ignored the comment, hoping he'd realize I just wasn't interested.

I continued. He mentioned massaging me again. And again.

"I'm sorry, I don't offer that," I said with a smile.

"That's a shame," he said.

I heard "that's a shame" quite a bit in this business. Do you offer full service? That's a shame. Do you do fully nude? Shame. Will you masturbate with toys in front of me? It's all a terrible shame.

"I wish you would let me massage you. I'd do a great job," he said.

"I'm sure you would," I said. "But I'm sorry."

And with that, his member deflated. I attempted resuscitation, to no avail. I have learned that true switchers generally can't get off without massaging the woman.

After our session, I re-revised all my ads to include, "No switching."

54

MS. MARKETING PANTS

Yesterday morning, right after I finished up with a client, I heard the ever-so-slight tap on the door.

I opened the door and it was Cecilia, smiling, looking almost sheepish. She was a massage therapist in the building and she and I had the only two studios on the third floor. As one walked up the staircase, to the left was my studio and to the right was Cecilia's. Just like in the studio with Maura, Cecilia didn't exactly have a steady stream of clients and again, I attempted to keep interactions to a minimum.

"I saw your client leave, so I figured it was safe to knock," she said. "I have a question to ask."

Instant nausea. *What's that odd moaning coming from your studio?*

"Karen and I are interested in advertising on LivingSocial and we need a third masseuse." LivingSocial is a website that offers "daily deals with discounts of up to 90 percent at local restaurants, bars, spas, theaters, and more."

According to Cecilia, LivingSocial required three masseuses to register because the response was generally so high that they wanted to make sure all respondents could be accommodated. The purchaser had one year to redeem.

Cecilia usually charged $70 for a massage, and on LivingSocial she would've offered $35, of which LivingSocial would take 50 percent, leaving a minuscule $17.50 for an hour-long Shiatsu massage. *Screw that.*

Cecilia acknowledged it wasn't much money, but it was a way to get a lot of new faces through the door.

"It sounds great, but I have a pretty full practice right now," I said.

Her eyes widened. "Really?"

I clenched my teeth, hoping she'd just spin on her heels and go back to her studio.

"Where do you advertise?" she asked, taking a step closer, leaning against the doorframe of my room.

I really need to rehearse my spiel. "I used to work for a chiropractor and he refers people to me."

"I see," she said, wheels turning, head nodding, and biting her lip.

"So, where did you go to school?" I gave her the same story I gave Maura.

"In Pennsylvania. I used to live there. And then I just had to take the exam when I moved here," I said.

"They made you take nationals over?" she asked, suddenly standing up straight.

Oh, shit, I really had no idea how that worked.

"Um, yeah, didn't you have to be fingerprinted?" I asked. I remembered reading that somewhere.

"No, I was grandfathered in. So, where did you work before here?"

I gave her the name of the complex I used to share with Maura.

"Do you know Maura and Jeanine?" Cecilia asked.

Damn, everyone seems to know everyone in this town.

"I shared a space with Maura."

Then Cecilia proceeded to tell me that Maura had asked to share studio space with Cecilia. Brother, what next, Ms. Bossypants and Ms. Nosypants moving in downstairs?

The advantage of moving from studio to studio in a sublease situation was to prevent anyone from accumulating enough data to verify my licensure (or lack thereof).

I'm fairly certain Maura had no clue, because she could have easily used her suspicions to justify keeping my security deposit. Instead, she simply complained that the head rest on the bed no longer retracted and that there was a waxy substance on her blanket (likely candle wax, and not from me).

And just when I thought it couldn't get worse, Cecilia added, "Just let me know if you'd like to trade." Now that I was down with the massage lingo, I knew she meant trade massages.

Up until this point, I had felt pretty good about possibly staying in the space I shared with Gwen, maybe even renewing our six-month agreement. The building had a variety of wellness practitioners, all of whom minded their own business, including Sally, a grandmotherly type on the first floor. As long as I brought in my fair share of toilet paper, no one bothered me. I had even been lucky enough to not raise an eyebrow when a couple of the other suitemates saw me in a blonde wig. Cecilia had yet to see me as a blonde.

I hoped Cecelia came up with a better way to bring in new business. Although business would mean she'd be there more often, as well as a steady stream of coupon-clipping clients. Then my space wouldn't be so private anymore. I'd hate to muffle a guy when he was in the midst of his O face. Now that would've been bad business.

55

A HAPPY ACCIDENT

Pierre immediately seemed like a good client because he was friendly and polite. He did not ask questions like "What is your bra size?" or "Can I stare?"

Pierre had long, gray hair tied into a short ponytail. I'm not partial to the look, but on him, it worked.

I have a theory that the younger the guy, the farther their ejaculate shoots. Old men dribble; young guys require a hazmat team. As a body rubber, this was a salient observation to minimize post-session blacklight inspections.

Pierre's face looked to be in his early fifties, his body to be in its early forties. Pierre was a fit bicyclist who had lived his life in Colorado. Avid Colorado bicyclists usually had amazing quads and ass due to the terrain, but given the elevation and days of Colorado sunshine, also had sun-baked skin that resembled a well-worn leather handbag.

Pierre discussed how long he had lived in Colorado, and I quickly realized he was even older than I thought. A dribbler for sure. No need to worry about aim, interception with a hand towel, or getting it in his eye (or mine).

With ten minutes left, I went to work on his release. And then suddenly, it was as if someone turned on a hose at full force, releasing a tremendous amount of pressure. I wielded his wiener to minimize collateral damage to the bookshelf filled with books, knickknacks, and other things with miniscule crevices. I aimed off to the side and heard a thwack as if someone had just dropped a gold bullion on the carpet.

I didn't say a word. It was my policy. I didn't comment on bodies— unless they are notably nice—or performance (not that it's really a "performance").

Pierre sat up, looking flush and winded.

"Wow."

"Feel better?" I asked.

"Amazing. Did that hit the floor?"

"I think it did."

Still naked, Pierre scrambled off the table and began searching on the floor. I looked down at the dark, Berber carpet. I expected to see a puddle, but it was impossible to discern any staining. My plan was to do a complete steam clean. The carpets needed it anyway. Pierre claimed that ten years earlier he'd had sex with another masseuse in this very room. If the walls could talk!

Pierre got down on all fours and used his palm to search for the wet spot, giving me a view of the back of his hanging testicles. Remember that frustrating game, Kerbangers? I was never quite able to get the hang of it.

"We wouldn't want anyone to step on it," he said, practically under the table at this point.

I was touched, really. I mean, *this* was chivalry. My clients, almost without exception, were very considerate when it came to their ejaculate, asking me where I wanted the washcloths. I opened the laundry bag and they dropped them in. (Incidentally, I used latex gloves when I did the laundry, followed up with scalding hand washing and hand sanitizer. Rinse. Repeat. The skin on my hands now resembles Pierre's face.)

Pierre's level of consideration was unprecedented and quite welcomed. I liked his matter-of-fact way of tackling bodily fluids, and then I remembered that he said he worked in an ER.

"I found it!" he exclaimed, still on all fours, one palm over the spot like he was playing Twister. He looked up at me like he had found my lost diamond earring.

"Here, put a washcloth over it and I'll use the rug shampoo," I said.

If Pierre booked again, I'd roll out the (plastic) red carpet for him. And next time I rented a studio, I'd look for a wipeable floor covering.

56

TEXTING DON'TS

I received a call from Grant, who responded to my body rub ad. Our schedules didn't coincide for that particular day, but he had some questions. One was if I took "old guys." *Of course.* Then he wanted me to explain a little bit about my services.

"I offer a *full* body rub with you naked and me topless. I allow some touching, but not mutual massage. I offer what you would get if you went to Boulder Sensations or a massage parlor." (With this, 95 percent of guys got the picture.)

Grant seemed satisfied with my response and said he'd call back the next time he was close. He lived in an animal butchering town approximately forty-five minutes away.

The next time he called, we booked an early afternoon appointment. After I finished up with my noon appointment, I turned my phone back on and found that Grant had left a voice message indicating he would likely be thirty minutes late. He also left a subsequent text: "On my way."

By my estimates, he would be forty-five minutes late and I had another person booked after him. I usually left fifteen minutes between clients. If a person was five or ten minutes late, no problem. If he was thirty minutes late, then I offered a thirty-minute session. I couldn't accommodate forty-five minutes tardiness, plus it didn't bode well for a respectful business relationship.

As I was ready to call him back to cancel—did he think he was my only client?—I got this text: "Just to be clear, I am wanting a sensual massage with xtras."

Brother. Now why did he have to go and do that?

In addition to the stupidity of putting such a thing in a text, the tone felt a little demanding to me. What were "xtras"? Most men understood that a sensual massage included a release, nudity, and some mutual touching. But a small percentage of rub girls offered more. I didn't and clients with these expectations were generally a pain in the pussy.

I decided Grant had wasted enough of my time and called my subsequent appointment, an anesthesiologist, to let him know that someone canceled and he could come early if he wanted. He did and said he'd be there shortly.

After I finished up with the doc, I turned my phone back on and received this text from Grant: "Since you didn't answer, I am assuming you are charging $125 for a regular massage? Which is very high."

Duh, no kidding, it is high, which is an indication that it's more than a regular massage. Some people just couldn't read between the sheets. Grant was promptly put on the "No" list.

57

WHO TO TAKE TO THE PROM

I was scheduled to undergo Lasik surgery which would take place in the fall, and which was a procedure entirely paid for by hand jobs—twenty-two, to be exact. I needed someone to drop me off, wait around until the Valium took effect, and then bring me home since I'd have pirate-eye patches. I believed this was a job for the closest thing I had to a boyfriend: Boy Friday. Although Boy Friday was meant for good times, I figured it was a small request.

When I mentioned my surgery and that I couldn't drive myself home, Boy Friday balked, claiming he had to check his work schedule. He took his job very seriously. He was a barista; yes, that's right, just a fancy name for a coffee cashier. You'd think he was the only over-educated grad who knew how to make a skinny latté.

The next day I asked Boy Friday, "Did you check your schedule?"

"I *guess* I can take you," he said while eating chips on my sofa. He knew how I was about crumbs, particularly on my new sofa. *Was this part of the negotiation?* "How long will it take?"

Brother. "An hour including check-in. It's just twenty seconds per eye."

Boy Fridays, in general, were all about fun, and wanted no boyfriend/husband responsibilities, such as medical transport. However, was an hour really too much to ask? He could've played with his damn phone the entire time.

Although Boy Friday reluctantly agreed, I couldn't help but think of other options, such as a client I had grown closer to, one I had a slight crush on. He was a regular that I saw quite frequently, perhaps more than any other client. He was single with no kids. He worked long hours, so he preferred to be my last appointment. Being the last session of the day was also a way that we could extend our time because I didn't have another client afterwards. On nights I worked, it was either talk with him after a session or go home to an empty house. He didn't have anyone to go home to, either, and he had made his feelings for me known.

A relationship wasn't possible, but a trip to Lasik might've been. He wouldn't even have complained, despite the fact that his working hours were far better compensated than Mr. Barista.

Asking this client if he would take me would've brought things to a whole new dimension. One in which I would not be wearing makeup. One in which I might have allowed an unfiltered comment to slip in my Valium-induced state. I had a few weeks to decide whether I could ask him.

58

Too Close to the Heat

I didn't work too many evenings, but on the rare occasions that I did, I lit candles. It sounds romantic, but the candles served a double purpose. My studio was woefully dim (no overhead lights and a lack of outlets for lamps). I also felt more vulnerable at night. The building tended to vacate as it got dark; the only one working at night was the clairvoyant on the first floor. In the unlikely possibility of booking Craigslist Killer #2, I could've thrown a lit candle or two on him. And then maced him. It was a one-two approach likely to have left a big mess in the carpeted studio. Luckily, I hadn't left a security deposit.

One unseasonably cool September day just before a session, I turned on the space heater that was on a shelf. The space heater was close to a couple dozen never-used ivory candles.

The landlord was a real cheap ass and the thermostat was controlled by an Oz-like creature in the building. I believed it was the same unknown who did the cleaning, or didn't do it, but supposedly got a break on rent for claiming he did. Even the clairvoyant didn't know who controlled the heat (or the cleaning). Space heaters were the only option.

By the time my session was over, about a dozen candles had melted to the shelf, with only their pristine wicks standing erect. I needed a sharp edge to clean it up and figured I'd do it later. Later turned into a couple weeks. My studio-sharer, Gwendolyn, caught sight of the situation and naturally assumed that I'd chosen to light a dozen candles simultaneously on a burnable surface. This would have been remarkable considering none of the wicks had black tips. I don't think Gwendolyn was the brightest bulb, but she certainly was a feisty one.

She left the following note:

Dear Melissa,

It's clear that you've been burning candles directly on the shelf instead of inside a candle holder. I know for a fact that this is a fire/safety hazard, which is a direct violation of your lease. Please use a candle holder to burn candles (instead of a flammable surface!) or I will have to ask you to remove all candles.

Have a nice day!
Gwendolyn

Gwendolyn seemed affable when we first met, but had a bitchy edge that she seemed to unleash readily. I'd seen her leave nasty notes for the landlord because he'd asked her to pay her unpaid balance (she wasn't very good at math, either). I'd heard that she'd come unglued because there wasn't any toilet paper in the bathroom. So it should have come as no surprise that she'd treat me the same. The frustrating thing about such a person was that, if she misjudged so hastily about the melted candles, how would she have reacted if she found me out? She didn't strike me as the type that would've suggested we part ways and leave it at that. She was a squasher; one who needed to punish others to even out a universal scorecard she'd fallen short on.

To Gwen's credit, once I explained the space heater mishap in a note, she apologized, claiming that she saw the melted candles and became "instantly alarmed."

Since I'd signed the six-month sublease, which extended to December, I hadn't even seen Gwen. I left my portion of the rent, she left a receipt, and I made sure that I allowed plenty of time between her last appointment and my first.

I paid the majority of the rent because I was there the most, but Gwen acted like she owned the studio because she was there first and had the lease with the owner, albeit a month-to-month lease.

My hope of continuing to rent the space lessened the more I got to know Gwen. Based on the feedback I received from my blog post, "What Are My Chances of Getting Arrested," my biggest threat was someone who filed a complaint against me. I wasn't trafficking, employing other girls, or prostituting on the streets, but if someone were to complain to the police, well then, the cops might just have to check it out.

No more six-month sublets with the Gwens, Mauras, Nosypants, and Bossypants of the world, I decided. I'd either go solo or month-to-month. Unfortunately, there wasn't a lot of availability for massage studios.

59

WHEN SUGAR DADDY GETS TOO STICKY

One morning, while rinsing the shampoo from my hair, I had an overwhelming feeling of dread. It was Monday and that meant a double pop with Martin (i.e., Sugar Daddy). To recap, Martin was my sixty-something, smoking (not the hot kind) client who patronized me at least weekly with a happy beginning and ending. Sugar Daddy had offered a special arrangement of sex in exchange for being on his payroll. I'd declined, but we'd continued our body rubs.

In the beginning, I looked forward to his appointments; he was familiar and a great conversationalist. Then, during our last appointment, I noticed the ever-so-slight tone of control, like the one a significant other exerts. "You should do this . . . you shouldn't do that . . ." less jokingly than before, and with an edge.

The enjoyment of our sessions waned when Martin went in for a kiss on the lips upon departing. Usually I gave clients a hug. Since he was so familiar, I leaned in to allow a kiss on the cheek, but suddenly

I couldn't avoid his lips on mine, which was his intention. Now that he had set the precedent of a frontal kiss, it became customary. And I hated it. Did I mention he was a smoker? And the same age as my dad? Did I mention the words "gobble, gobble" came to mind when he puckered up and leaned down?

Even the most stimulating of intellects could not compensate for unwanted physical contact. I was okay with a hand job—or two—but kissing, even a peck on the lips, felt intimate. He knew this; we'd discussed it in other situations, just not *our* kissing.

Because of his escort experiences in California, he was accustomed to things I did not provide—yet deep down, he wanted those things. By staying my client, he knew he wouldn't get them. I think he couldn't help but resent that. And I resented his resenting.

"How is your boyfriend?" he asked one morning, after he dropped his drawers and took off the nylons that helped his varicose veins.

I was honest with Martin, less guarded than with others simply because I saw him often. He believed Boy Friday to be boyfriend, which was an overstatement, but I always told clients I had a boyfriend.

"Not so well," I said.

"I figured," he said, having never liked Boy Friday from what little bits I had shared. "Just don't use this venture for finding a boyfriend."

"I wouldn't date someone I met here."

"But you did," he said with a mirthless guffaw. Cotton Candy Guy. The date had been so lackluster that I had already forgotten.

"I guess I should say that I would never *again* date someone I met here," I said.

"And never tell anyone what you do for a living," he said, gesticulating with a sideways karate chop as he lay face up on the massage table.

Too late, I'd told a couple people. And really, who was he to tell me what to do?

"And always tell clients you have a boyfriend," he continued.

I switched the subject to his Estes Park weekend foliage trip with his wife and the Amanda Knox trial. The last thing I wanted was my life under scrutiny. I also didn't follow directions very well.

I went to work on his happy beginning, and he closed his eyes and was silent. Although he prided himself on being able to come twice within the hour and a half, it didn't happen easily. He took twice as long as most; afterwards, I felt like I needed to ice my arm. He paid me $150 for our session and occasionally tipped another ten to thirty dollars, which was slightly less than a full-service escort. Despite the fact that he could get anything he wanted for a slightly higher price, he had told me repeatedly that he was glad he had found me. He had come to me first, tried others, and then came back.

Like his torso, his penis had a lot of excess skin along with age-related softening during an erection; a good rhythm was difficult. A mis-stroke could have resulted in a painful bend. The head of his penis also happened to be abnormally large and glossy, like a forest mushroom after a dewy rain. I was tired of looking at it. I had to look at it for no less than thirty minutes every week while I listened to his crescendo of "Oh, oh." Most men were not this vocal.

If he wasn't looking, I'd divert my eyes and make anagrams out of labels in the studio. Did you know the word urine can be formed from Eucerin (as in the lotion)?

After he finally came, he composed himself, licked his lips and asked me how business had been.

"Great, it's been picking up since summer ended," I said. Then I mentioned that I was thinking of planning an overseas trip to a country where body rubs were legal and the income would be good. A place I had never been and wanted to go.

"Such as?" he asked.

"Maybe London. Have you been there?" I asked.

"For body rubs or more?" he asked, wide-eyed.

"Just body rubs," I said.

"Oh, you scared me there for a second," he said.

And so what if I did? None of his business.

Martin was the one who warned me, in a lengthy e-mail, not to go any further in this business, yet had propositioned me for a sex-for-money relationship. Somehow, that was different to him. The concern for my welfare was a touch endearing in the beginning, but quickly grew irritating. He either wanted to be the first to know, so he could be the first, or he felt the need to exert control over yet another sex worker. He claimed to have a lengthy history of helping escorts in getting sober, organizing their finances, opening their first checking account, sending care packages to them while in jail (for drugs), and even paying a subsidy to one so that she could quit escorting and stay faithful just to him. For girls who needed rescuing, he was a White Knight. I, however, was not a distressed damsel. Or so I thought.

60

THE MEAT-PACKING ESCORT:
PAY IT FORWARD

One Saturday, one of my clients awoke with a "boner" and a "burning desire for Melissa." He texted me, and upon learning that I was not working that weekend, he pounced on Backpage to find a substitute.

James was single and not a proactive dater. Instead he opted for escorts and body rubbers to fulfill his desires. He came to me nearly weekly, but that morning he opted to seek an escort.

James described her pictures as enticing. Her ad described an ethnic beauty with curves and an angelic face with sweet, pouty lips. She appeared to be in her late twenties, an age that wasn't too young for fifty-five-year-old James, but younger than anything he'd be able to get on his own.

He called to book and she was eager to take his appointment. He heard her turn away from the phone and tell someone to hold on, she'd be right with him. She was booked all day but had some evening appointments. None of the other providers he contacted had returned his calls, so he went with it, even though she was a drive out of town.

Personally, I think nothing good happens in a town that's known for its crowded, filthy feedlots and stinks of manure and animal entrails. Despite that and with a hanky—for the smell—in hand, James made the trip to a nearby town that isn't exactly known as a tourist hotspot.

James's exotic beauty didn't require any screening, but she used the two-call system where she'd text him one location, then once he got there, she'd text another location. Most escorts use the two-call system, which ensures that the first client has left the premises before the next one arrives to ensure clients a measure of privacy. In Angelic Escort's case, a ten text system was used to reach the final destination. The series of texts took James on a loop of feedlots and turkey-butchering plants. Perhaps she was busy with another client and hoping to stall him. The notion of patronizing an escort back-to-back with another dude was generally a big turn-off to most men and was reason enough to spin on one's heels back to the car.

Once James finally arrived at the final location, he looked around at the rundown apartment building. The property was barren of greenery except weeds creeping from the cracked asphalt. Debris scattered the lot.

He walked up the stairs, practically tripping over a guy slumped over on the landing, and with the final text, she gave him the apartment number. Even before he went in, he could see that the door was broken off the hinge. He knocked and what answered was far from what he had imagined.

Perhaps sixty pounds heavier than her pictures, she looked beat and a glazed donut-like smear was encrusted into her cheek and hair. She wore black tights with more runners than not, a hot pink tank, and a denim skirt so short that enough slack was improbable for lady-like sitting.

"Do you want to come in?" she asked.

James stepped inside, and the apartment was dirty, worn, and cluttered with kids' toys. He described it as a dive.

"She hadn't even tidied up?" I asked, incredulous.

"Nope," he said.

I've heard the scenario repeatedly from men: The incall location was the girl's residence and it was dirty and cluttered. Perhaps even more disturbing was the presence of other people or children.

If James described a place as a dive, I believed it to be horrendous. He described his own place as a one-bedroom basement apartment full of boxes because he cleaned out his storage locker. (How long ago? Months!) His roommate was "Ms. Pickles," a calico who came and went out a window accessed by a propped-up ironing board. One time James came home to find Ms. Pickles and a future Mr. Pickles hanging out in his living room. James was single and had said that he could live in a cave and be completely satisfied. I believed him, because it sounded like he lived in a cave, and I knew he could afford more.

"My son's sleeping," the escort said.

James looked around and became so depressed about how the child was living, his future, and his mother that his desire deflated. He gave her $50 and told her he couldn't go through with it. She brightened. "Thank you," the escort said, and then he left.

That'll teach him to cheat on me.

61

IS A HAPPY-ENDING MASSAGE CHEATING?

M̲ost people have a quick response to this question, and often a passionate one, particularly the wives who discover their spouse's extracurricular activities. To many of these wives, body-rub girls are whores that are breaking apart families. I can understand the rage, but I think it's misdirected. Take away all the sex workers of the world, and all men won't suddenly become faithful. Others argue it's not an issue of being faithful, it's a fun excursion.

This debate played out on the comment section of the popular blog, *HappyEndingz: Confessions of an Erotic Masseuse*. This blog has been around for years and has a considerable following. And with any large audience comes the haters. Unlike me, the author, C.J., allows unfiltered comments, so anyone can post immediately, thus giving everyone free mud-slinging reign. Perhaps my skin isn't as thick as C.J.'s because any comment that begins with "whore" or a similar pejorative, usually with lots of exclamation points, gets deleted before I read the whole thing or it is posted to my blog. I feel everyone is entitled to their opinion, but I'm the one paying for and providing the platform, so the haters can go elsewhere or start their own blog.

Based on what I could glean from C.J.'s married commenter, she was trying to keep her husband, kids and home happy and then she discovered he had been cheating via erotic massages and likely more. She went on a hunt to discover more about this happy ending stuff, came across C.J.'s blog, and decided to give her a cyber lashing. I shortened the comment for the sake of succinctness.

Well I hate to admit it, but I became the VICTIM of a cheating husband who visited parlors. We've always had a great marriage and super sex. He wanted it anytime, anywhere. So imagine my surprise when I discovered his visits to these places. My anger led me to your blog. I am shocked at your nonchalance. What about the wives at home working their fingers to the bone to keep happy house, happy kids, and very happy husband? Why are you ignoring the fact that this is illegal, immoral, and devastating to families—especially the children who lose their fathers? I don't know you and by no means want to direct my anger towards you, because the fault lies mostly with the husbands, but explain to me why this is ok?

This is prostitution. Ok, you're not having sex, but they are climaxing between your fucking tits and ass? Something to be reserved for the great wives who give their husbands everything they need sexually. Don't you feel bad at all?

Money's one thing, but what about the devastation you cause once you're finished wiping the tenth client of the day's jiz off your face? What about the wife who is at home with a hot meal waiting for him and a blow job to boot? Or the dick that was just up your ass? No guilt? No feelings of "Hey, I wouldn't want to be his wife and what would I do if I were?" Again, I don't know you personally and as you can probably tell, I am a writer also.

What goes around, comes around. You're going to fall in love, head over heels, give up this horrible job, have children, and one day look at your husband's credit card and see a parlor on there. Maybe *worse—catch him with a girlfriend or a hooker. I hope I did my best in not making this against you, but more of a "hey help me out with this." Maybe the next time you have some guy's dick in your face in his wife's bedroom, looking at his kids' pictures, you'll think of me and the broken families this leaves. :(*

First of all, not all clients were married and obviously I didn't ask. In my studio, it was a "Don't Ask, Don't Tell" policy. However, I certainly thought of the wives, particularly in situations where the client was excessively pushy, such as Mark or Travis, or he had an addiction, such as Martin. It really wasn't my place to judge. The client was an adult; he could make his own decisions. When I worked at a convenience store during college, I sold cigarettes. I also sold alcohol to homeless people who came into the store. It wasn't my place to make decisions for people then and it wasn't my position to do so as a body-rub girl.

Most married men probably believe happy endings are cheating, otherwise they wouldn't be so paranoid and secretive. However, I doubt many clients felt any real connection to me or any other masseuse, although I have been told this is likely an incorrect assumption. In general, conversation was limited to exchanging daily pleasantries. Most didn't attempt to pursue a relationship, although there were exceptions. Men don't need the emotional or intellectual connection that most women do to get off.

Once, I received a phone call from Lisa, who started out by saying she needed to have an "awkward" conversation with me.

"My fiancé had your phone number in his phone. He contacted you a few months ago," she said.

"OK," I responded.

"You mentioned different rates for wearing lingerie, being topless or fully nude," she said in a halting tone. She paused as if she expected me to balk at the absurdity of what she was suggesting.

I was silent, waiting for her to continue.

"Is this a regular massage?" she asked.

"It's a body rub," I said, hoping she'd get the picture. If a woman has gotten to the point of searching her fiancé's phone and discovering correspondence between said fiancé and his body rub girl, it's time to rethink the relationship, not call the body rub girl in the hopes of allaying her fears. Yet, I felt sorry for her and wanted her to know enough of the truth to make a decision about her relationship, but not enough specifics to incriminate myself.

"I know about those happy ending massages. Is that what this is?" she asked.

Obviously, this is not a question I will ever answer over the phone because I do not want to end up in jail.

"All I can say is that I'm not exactly taking off my bra for the therapeutic aspects of the massage," I said.

She laughed, then proceeded to give me her fiancé's name and asked if I had seen him.

"Most men don't give their real names," I said.

She described him as beefy, toweringly tall, with bleached hair resembling some sort of reality cooking show star.

"Doesn't sound familiar," I said, which it didn't. He definitely wasn't a regular. "Good luck."

"Thanks," she said in a resigned-sounding tone.

The exchange showed that he clearly believed it was cheating, and so did she.

Some posters on my blog had strong feelings that erotic massage was not cheating because it simply filled a sexual void in the marriage and emotions were not involved. In many cases, there was no attraction to the masseuse; perhaps she was a fifty-something Asian woman who barely spoke English. Many men complained that if they received touch more often from their wives, they wouldn't have sought erotic massage. To the rationalizers, it was just a step above masturbation. Of course, this only represented one view of the marriage.

Another interesting comment came from an independent erotic masseuse, who was insulted by the married poster. Like me, the masseuse felt it was not her place to judge clients. She asserted that erotic massage could actually improve a marriage, where the husband received the touch he craved and then it didn't become an issue in the marriage. Client complaints of "not getting any" at home were ubiquitous. Married clients claimed body rubs were a resolution for many men who had unmet physical needs and didn't want a divorce. The erotic massage poster also claimed that one of her clients, a former marriage counselor, began slipping her number to his male patients. The former marriage counselor claimed the masseuse's work happily put him out of business, whereby he returned to his love of teaching.

On another level, there's the ick factor of parlors. Happy-ending massages are relatively unfamiliar to most women and the notion of a stranger putting his hands on her vagina is repulsive. In the case of escorts, disease is certainly a credible concern. I'm amazed that with Martin's decades of daily escort patronage, his body wasn't completely covered with weeping sores.

If nothing else, I think we can all agree that the angry poster's husband was the world's biggest dumb ass for charging his erotic massage. She might be better off without him.

62

On My Knees

Dear God,

I know it's quite likely that you are not too happy with me these days. We don't talk, I don't write, I don't go to church, I don't pray, and I do questionable things to earn a living. Despite all that, I'd like to make a request. You're *God* so I figure you don't hold a grudge against my backsliding.

One of my rentals is up for sale. Yes, *that* one, God. The house that continues to be a financial drain and source of anxiety. The home with a leaky roof, old sewer line, and a history of bad tenants, including a family who snuck in an unneutered cat, thus soaking the home in cat piss. I've sunk tens of thousands of dollars into meeting my financial obligation to the bank. And now, I just want the nightmare to be over.

I make this request now because there is an open house this weekend. I know chances are slim that an offer will come from it. I'm just going to hope, pray, and plead. And since my realtor is no longer taking my calls, I naturally thought of you. If I don't get an offer soon, I'll have to find new tenants when my current ones move out in a few months—which means I'll have to commit to another year of landlordship.

If you do this for me, God, I'll do something for you. With just a little more assistance in the job realm, I could get out of the business of hand jobs. Okay, so I guess that's two requests. But really, what I'm asking is just to be free of the rental that pushed me into erotic massage. That might be overstating things a tad, but it was a big factor. Please, God, free me from landlord purgatory, and I'll pound the pavement for a nice office job. Promise.

Love, me (on my knees).

FALL

63

BOY FRIDAY'S TAKE

Boy Friday and I went out for Thai food one cold autumn night. After our wine and beer arrived, I asked, "Did you know that some massage parlors offer hand jobs?"

"You mean happy endings?" he asked, after he swallowed.

"Yes."

"I'm from New Jersey, of course I do. Those places are everywhere," he said, raising one eyebrow. "Why do you ask?"

"Just curious. I read something in the paper about them," I said. Boy Friday didn't read the paper so I knew there'd be no who-and-what questions regarding the article.

"Are you trying to ask me if I've ever been to one?" he asked, leaning in with a smile. "Because I haven't, in case you were wondering."

"I wasn't wondering, really," I said. "But don't you think it's strange, in a way? I mean, as a woman, I just can't imagine going into a place of business to be finger-fucked by a guy, one who might be unattractive."

"I know some guys who went, back when I was in the army. I was never a part of it. I just didn't like the idea of some random chick jerking me off," he said.

Happy-ending massages weren't exactly in Boy Friday's current budget, either.

"Were any of those guys who went, your friends, were they married?"

"Of course. Who do you think goes to those kinds of places? I bet the majority of men who go there are married."

Boy Friday still didn't know what I did for a living. I told him I was a freelancer and he wasn't much more curious than that.

"Do you think it's cheating? Assuming the person is with someone?" I said.

He also didn't generally have strong opinions about things that didn't affect him, so it was surprising to hear his quick response.

"Absolutely," he said, wide-eyed. "Anything you do in secret, sexually, is cheating."

This was a conversation I was thinking more women needed to have with their significant others.

"Don't you think?" he asked, finally warm enough that he took off his coat.

"I do, I definitely do. I just know some men don't think of it as cheating."

"If they didn't think it was cheating, then they would tell their wives. I can guarantee you that none of my army friends went home and told their wives about the happy ending they got," he said. "That just goes to show that they believe it's cheating, despite what they tell themselves and others." He jabbed the air with his finger.

Hmm, interesting. Maybe Boy Friday was more of a keeper than I had thought. Because, for me, a body rub was cheating.

64

FALL BACK

In September I finally admitted that summer was over. I dragged out the winter clothes from the garage.

Business picked up this month, thankfully. The new identities helped get me through the summer, but there were only so many girls I could be. Almost everyone wanted an appointment *after* work, with the peak requests between 4 p.m. and 8 p.m. Perhaps the fragile economy prevented patrons from taking an extended lunch to jerk around midday. When men left my studio, they looked dazed, in some cases drugged, and moved *very* slowly. Some clients had mentioned mentally replaying our session for the rest of the day. I couldn't imagine that was very productive for computer programming. This burst of worker efficiency was botching my workday. My workweek had generally consisted of weekdays, two weeknights, and every other Saturday, but now I was working more evenings. As a body-rub girl, I learned I had to go with the flow, particularly since I still wasn't getting any response from jobs I had applied to.

65

PAVLOV'S PENIS

One morning, I broke my living room window as I attempted to stick a suction-cup cat toy to already cracked glass. Then, about an hour later, after I had been ignoring my "check engine" light for two months, my car broke down.

Left with nothing but my 1970s Schwinn for transport, I biked to my afternoon appointment. I bought the bike at a garage sale, and the gears started slipping almost immediately. Like the car, I ignored it, believing it didn't require my immediate attention.

That afternoon, I was in the bike lane and a college student was in front of me, biking slowly with a viola on her back. Just as I attempted to pass her, on a slight incline, the gears slipped, throwing me off balance and onto the pavement, ripping my jeans at the knee and taking the skin along with it.

"Are you okay?" the violist asked, having stopped to look down at my crumpled form.

"Yes, thanks for stopping," I said, running my tongue over my front teeth to make sure they were still there.

"That happened to me once," the violist said, as she adjusted her instrument and then pedaled off.

Losing skin on the knee made me appreciate epidermal elasticity. I got back on the bike, and every downward pedal felt as though I was tearing more skin.

My appointment was with Jeremy the Banker. He was a regular, coming every week or two. He wasn't much of a talker and generally easy to please, but I felt an oozing wound would need some explanation. Not so, apparently, when the breasts were on display. All attention went there. I had to do the body slide on one knee, thus cramping my left butt cheek.

After a couple appointments, I decided to go home, feeling I had caused enough destruction for the day.

When Boy Friday called later that evening, he asked how my day had been. I told him, hoping for assistance with my car, bike, or window. Instead, he suggested I needed a drink and would be right over with a bottle. That's Boy Friday for you. He's a drink of wine.

We made dinner, drank, talked, and had a pleasant evening. In addition to my weeping wound, I had a sore throat and suggested we go to bed early. Given my illness, sex was not an option. It's difficult to kiss when one has a stuffed-up nose, and sex without kissing is about as intimate as a body rub.

As always, as soon as Boy Friday hit the bed, he got an instant boner. Seriously, Pavlov's dog had nothing on Boy Friday when it came to classical conditioning. Luckily, he didn't have intercourse aspirations; he understood that I wasn't up to the task. He was probably only staying over because he had had alcohol and was cautious of driving, having had a problem with that in the past.

"Uh-oh," Boy Friday said, as he lifted the sheet to show me his erection.

"Wow, impressive. That's a shame," I said, rolling over.

"Can you give me a hand job?" he asked.

For $120 I will.

I had given Boy Friday hand jobs in the past and generally it took *forever*. I think because his penis knew that it usually got better service, it just didn't cooperate with a mere hand job.

"Can't you do it yourself?" I asked.

"It's not the same," he whined.

I know. It's the difference between free and $120.

"Let's wait until the morning," I said. I was asleep ten minutes later.

At about 3 a.m., he nudged me and in a hushed tone said, "I have to go."

"Why?" I asked, sitting up in the darkness.

"I can't sleep because of my hard-on," he said.

"Why don't you just jerk off?"

"I can't do that in front of you," he hissed.

Oh, trust me, yes, you can.

"Okay, just make sure you lock the door on the way out," I said, falling back to the bed. It must be difficult to let your genitals direct so much of your life.

The next day, I asked him if he had gone home to masturbate. Boy Friday didn't deny masturbation (believe it or not, some guys actually do) but he was sheepish when admitting it.

"No, it went away as soon as I got into my truck," he said.

"Then why didn't you just come back in after it went away?" I asked.

"Because it would've come back," he said. "From sleeping next to you."

Poor Boy Friday. I promised not to drive him out in the cold again.

66

THE NEW GIRL IN TOWN

In the beginning of October, my mother came to town for ten days, which threw a wrench in my system. It was difficult to answer my pre-paid cell phone with, "Melissa's Rub and Tug!" without raising an overplucked eyebrow. The ring of either one of my two body rub cell phones would've required an explanation, as my iPhone sat idly on the coffee table. Leaving these phones off while I was with my mother was another tough one because when most clients called, they wanted an appointment *now*, and I had a new window, new gear shifter, and car thermostat to pay for.

I'd been leaving my body rub phones in my pocket, and when they vibrated:

"It's going to freeze tonight. I'd better pick the last of the tomatoes!"

"I'm going to the garage to get the rest of the winter clothes."

"I need to clean out my car."

"Oh, please, let *me* take out the recyclables." (The wine bottles piled up when mom was in town.)

Upon delivering one of these lines, I'd dart outside and sit in the garage or in my car and answer the usual questions: How much do you charge? Do you do fully nude? Will I get a full release at the end? Will you come to my place? Apparently no one actually read the ads; it was just drool and dial.

After I had made an appointment, I'd tell my mother I had to go to the office. This was the office I used to work at quite a long time ago. I prayed that I never bumped into a previous co-worker while downtown having lunch with my mother. I wasn't sure how long I could keep up the farce. Maybe I needed to switch fake vocations.

My mother had become suspicious of my recent spending: Lasik, manicures, pedicures, Whole Foods, and laser hair removal. As I headed out the door to my acupuncture appointment, my coupon-clipping mother quipped, "Acupuncture? For what? Hmm, you just don't know what to spend your money on next." And then she went back to crocheting a baby blanket.

I wanted to blurt out that it was fine, I had more than enough to pay for such expenditures, but figured it wouldn't serve me well. Though I was much more financially well off than a year ago, I still needed body rub income to sustain my transition to another career. What career? I still didn't know.

During my mother's visit, I also became a Laundromat patron. I thought my mother might question why I came home from the "office" with large bags of laundry. And why I had more sheets and hand towels to fold than a Marriott. At the Laundromat also I was likely raising eyebrows, as I used my latex gloves to sort crusty hand towels. But as long as those eyebrows didn't belong to my Catholic and conventional mother, I was okay with it.

67

PROM DILEMMA SOLVED

I had a medical transport dilemma: Boy Friday or Client I Might Have A Crush On to take me to my Lasik procedure. I gave it much thought, and my blog readers heartily recommended selecting The Client. I leaned toward asking the client at our next weekly appointment.

I imagined him being flattered I was asking him to assist me, despite his busy schedule. I would be flattered that he was flattered and it would be the best of happy endings. On the day I was going to ask him, he decided to figure me out. What was a girl with a master's degree from a good family doing in a place like this? Doing *this*?

I didn't like to be figured out. I was Melissa when I was working. I went home and became Anna. Melissa was the girl who couldn't enough of men! Anna preferred a good book and her neutered cat to snuggle with. Trying to reconcile the two was like trying to get Sybil onboard with all her personalities.

It also pained me to have it pointed out that I was clearly over-educated (i.e., I have wasted my education) for the position I held.

Everything I needed to know I learned from Mark McDonald in the closet of Kelly's party in high school.

The key to analyzing me, according to my client, was understanding my relationship with Boy Friday.

"I don't understand how this doesn't bother your boyfriend," he said.

"It does," I said, as I opened up the laundry bag for him to drop his towels into. In my effort to establish a boundary, I always told clients that I had a boyfriend, and that this boyfriend knew that I did body rubs for a living. It wasn't true, but it was part of the life I had created for Melissa.

My client had asked this question before. He shook his head as I told him. I wished he would get off this subject.

And then he did it. He said what I've heard from so many other clients: If you were *my* girlfriend, I'd do anything in my power so that you wouldn't need to do this. And that would've essentially made me a kept woman. I understood that a guy wouldn't want his girlfriend to fondle male genitals all day, no matter how mechanical it was, but being on a guy's payroll would only have made me worse off.

Admittedly, I was entirely reliant on men to make a living. To begin dating the client and take him up on his offer would've made me reliant on *one* guy. Would you invest your entire retirement in the shares of one company? No! Diversify, diversify, diversify.

And let's just say, hypothetically, that I chose to date him and let him pay for everything, believing I could one day return to body rubs if we broke up. Let's say it went so well that I embarked on a new profession, having to earn some sort of credential first. If this client turned boyfriend happened to irk me, if I fell out of love with him, it wouldn't just be the end of our relationship; it would be a geologic shift of my lifestyle. Such potential shifts tend to make people stay put. Next thing I'd know, I'd be saddled with kids with colds, working as a dental assistant, and getting pissed when he charged his happy-ending massage.

I'd decided to keep Client I Might Have a Crush On as strictly a client, perhaps a little more, such as engaging in post-session drinks at a restaurant, but definitely not a boyfriend or a medical transporter. Some day, I hope, I might find a guy who motivates me enough to leave what I do, before I have to tell him what I do. And I'd never tell Future Boyfriend about my prior job.

In the end, Boy Friday took me to the appointment and I gave him an A+ on his fifteen minutes of acting like a boyfriend. He ignored my ramblings while on Valium: he propped up pillows, and lined up the artificial tears while my eye shields were on. It was uncomplicated and easy. Just how I liked it.

68

THE END OF SUGAR DADDY

One evening, as I was resting from a Halloween scavenger hunt, I received a series of texts from Martin (combined into one for clarity):

I'm going to have to quit, Baby. I adore you, and that's the problem. To not touch you, taste you, and kiss you, has become increasingly difficult for me. You are too attractive and I'm too physical. Passive sex is just not enough with someone like me, especially with someone like you. I hope you understand. I hope I remain your friend and I am available if you ever need advice or someone to talk to, but I have too much respect for you to take the risk of making you uncomfortable or alienating you due to my own proclivities and weakness. I realized last time that it is increasingly difficult for me to maintain control over my desire for you. Simple as that. Take Care.

I was relieved. I did not want to be put in the position of having to tell him he couldn't come back. I didn't want to be the one to break it off.

I liked him. He was intelligent, witty, caring and self-reflective. If I did not know him in my role as body-rub girl, I never would have seen the sex addict in him. And to be candid, any untreated addiction is ugly.

To watch him ooh and aah as I gave him his second hand job in the morning—a man old enough to be my father—was sickening. At our previous appointment, he'd had difficulty achieving orgasm at the second go-around. He told me he needed to stand up. He positioned himself behind me, masturbating with one hand and cradling my breast with the other, his orgasmic mutterings just inches from my ear. I attempted to zone out, imagining myself on a beach with my toes in the sand, not standing there with the saggy, nicotine-stained man fondling me.

After he came, he leaned down, kissed me on the top of my head, and breathed deeply as if to inhale the entirety of my smell, enough to last a week, until he returned.

I did not miss my weekly appointments with him. Though this decision meant the loss of a minimum $150 weekly, it wasn't worth it. In addition, there were plenty more where he came from. Despite my relief at his decision, it made me sad to think he was going back to escorts.

Perhaps most sad was the effect on his wife. While he was taking a vacation with one of his escorts-turned-girlfriends, Faithful Wife had learned of the affairs, and the escorts. When she confronted him, he confessed it all and, despite all that, she begged him not to leave her. He acknowledged that he did not understand his wife's undying love and she deserved much better. Body rubs versus full service was his compromise—an apparent attempt to mitigate marital damage. Apparently, his addiction could not be compromised.

A week later, an escort, Amanda, called to request a reference for Sugar Daddy. Most escorts required a reference before booking to determine a client's credibility.

"This is Amanda, I'm calling to check on a Martin Scovo," she said, using his number to confirm.

"He's great," I said. *Until he gets too attached.*

69

Cock Therapy

"Is my cock big enough?" Three o'clock asked. I don't like the word "cock," but that's what he kept calling it. His penis was, in fact, shockingly large, particularly given his stature, standing just a couple inches taller than I. And I am exceptionally short.

"Definitely," I said.

His abrupt question startled my wandering mind. While rubbing, I had been debating whether I should ask my downstairs tenants to help with the snow shoveling. By the beginning of November, two storms separated only a week apart brought two feet of snow. *Should I be responsible for shoveling all of the long driveway, the front steps, and the back steps and patio?* My back burned and those two girls were able-bodied. You would've thought placing the shovel by their back door would've been a big enough hint. Apparently not.

"Because sometimes I compare myself to the guys on porn and it makes me sad," Three o'clock said. I turned to face him and he was forcing a frown. He looked like a balding puppy with big brown eyes.

When the porn starts to make you sad, it's time to turn it off.

It was easy to tell the difference between porn addicts and the dabblers. The addicts had distorted ideas of what turned women on, loved lots of dirty talk, and thought I would enjoy having them come on my breasts. That sounded just as enjoyable as having someone with an upper respiratory infection sneeze on my chest.

The addicts were supercharged and bucking for something spicy, expecting our exchange to be something right out of the movies. Porn addicts also tended to be horrible lovers.

"Trust me, you are larger than average. I've seen a lot of really small penises and you are nowhere near that," I told him, hoping I could go back to figuring out exactly how to tell the girls downstairs that they needed to get off their asses and shovel. Maybe I could send them a text: "Feel free to use my shovel!"

"Have you ever had sex with a guy with a really large penis?" he asked.

"Yes," I said.

"I just worry that if a girl has had sex with a guy with a large cock and then has sex with me, she'll keep thinking it was better with the other guy," he said.

"There are a lot of factors that go into good sex other than penis size. Besides, you really do have a large cock," I said. "Trust me, I've seen a lot of them. I would know."

"I just want girls to *like* me," Three o'clock whined. He had gotten a divorce a couple years ago and claimed no one had touched him since. Until me.

I think the reason no one was touching him—for free—was due to other factors I had stumbled across in the session, such as a distorted sense of self. It wasn't my job to touch on those issues, however. I just handled the cocks.

70

THE WORLD'S WORST GUESSING GAME

My afternoon appointment placed his money on the table in my studio, tapped it with his pointer finger, and said, "I have something to discuss before we get started."

I raised an eyebrow, waiting for him to explain.

"I have a problem," he said.

"And?" I asked.

"Do you know what I'm talking about?" he asked. The man was ready to get naked and get a hand job. There was no need for shyness. And this sounded like the beginnings of the world's worst guessing game.

I hesitated. I had seen a lot of problems in my studio: crooked penises, missing prostates, and heavily forested junk. Perhaps most disturbing was toenail fungus. I would have rather serviced the elephant man with pristine toenails than Brad Pitt with thick, yellowed nails. If I had caught that, my pedicurist would have no longer seen me. And I would've had to hurt someone.

I figured he might've been talking about erectile dysfunction, but he needed to say it, not me. Instead, he kept silent and I wanted to get on with it.

"You can't get an erection?" I finally asked.

He nodded. "So I figured you were the person to come to," he said with a broad grin and arms outstretched like a preacher.

I didn't make the connection between what I did and correcting what was obviously something that needed medication or counseling. I felt for guys in this situation, but I was not *that* good. I couldn't correct deficient blood flow.

In addition, my extensive research revealed that the harder a man thought about it, the less likely he was to get erect. I have seen clients on the table ready to pop a forehead vein in the effort to get hard. It never worked. "Try, try, try," did not work with the penis. It had to happen naturally. When the body senses the will to harden, it will shut down. It does not appreciate such tomfoolery.

My opinions were based on experience. I was once engaged to a twenty-something guy who had a terrible problem getting it up. In the beginning, sex was spontaneous and splendid; then as our relationship developed, there was a complete penile flatline.

"It's not a big deal," I'd tell him. "It happens to all guys." And then it started to happen all the time. And after it did, he'd stomp around the house like a petulant child. It ruined many Saturday mornings.

For my ex-fiancé, I believed it was mental, which seemed more difficult to overcome. Mental can't be fixed with a pill, not in this case, anyway.

An ex-girlfriend had told him that he had a small penis. This tidbit was hurled at him in the midst of their breakup. He, unfortunately, carried this insult into our relationship, giving him quite the complex. He was big on knowing "my number."

"So, how many guys have you been with?" he had asked.

Why? So you can compare my number of sex partners with your number?

"You first," I said.

"I asked. You first," he said.

"You asked because you care. I don't care," I said. I had no doubt my number was higher.

My ex likely had a multitude of reasons why he wanted to know how many guys I had slept with. I think one of those reasons was to know how many penises I could compare his to. Frankly, I didn't care about the size of his penis; we had more important issues to deal with—and never dealt with. Thus the "ex."

We eventually broke up. He married and now has at least one child. All that was a long time ago. He still won't friend me on Facebook, the very last jab he can hurl through cyberspace for breaking off our engagement.

Remarkably, my client was able to conjure up some stiffness.

"You're doing it, you're doing it," he cheered me on as I stroked. I saw that familiar look of concentration and sensed impending failure.

After a few minutes, he said, "It's going down." He deflated before he was able to come. He sounded as if he had placed last in a race.

"It's not a big deal," I said. "It happens to all guys. Even the young ones."

71

I Corrupted a Saudi

My studio is in very close proximity to thousands of international students. These men, I have found, tend to be very good clients. They are young, often shy, and many times more liquid than the average college student. Apparently those rotary scholarships don't skimp.

In addition, international students as a group tend to be intelligent, inquisitive, and offer conversation that fast forwards time. And I enjoy the bits I gather from these countries. It's unlikely that I'll ever visit Qatar, but if I do, Client X assures me not to miss the Museum of Islamic Art. Who knew body rubs could provide such cultural insights?

My theory as to why I see more international students versus other 20-something students is that for one, these virile students might have a slightly harder time getting laid, given cultural barriers and such, and perhaps these students like to do a bit of sampling of the American culture. I might not have the same offerings as the Museum of Islamic Art, but the awe-inspired look on a Saudi's face when he's inches from my nipples likely rivals the unveiling of any Islamic art.

And so it went with Ishmael, who booked a one-hour appointment with me on a sunny afternoon just a week before engineering finals.

"I think you should know I've never seen a woman topless before," he said, electing to keep his baggy boxers on.

I hear a lot of crazy stuff, but this made me pause, particularly because I was just about ready to unfasten my bra. Do I or don't I?

"I'm from Saudi Arabia," he said. "You know Saudi, right?"

"Yes, I've heard of it." Those Saudis aren't messing around with that dress code.

Ishmael confirmed that indeed he wanted me to do the massage topless, his doe-like eyes practically popping out of his skull like those violent cartoons I watched as a kid when I removed my bra.

"Do men touch you?" he asked as I tried to massage the very little bit of him that was exposed. Although he was shirtless, he was a petite guy and his Ralph Lauren boxers reached down to his knees, and the waistband practically up to his chest. Ishmael reminded me of Maulik Pancholy from *Weeds*, although clearly not gay.

"You can touch me if you want," I told Ishmael.

With arms up in surrender as if I was pointing a loaded gun at him, he said, "Trust me, I wouldn't have the courage."

Though I felt like I was hardly doing any work, Ishmael enjoyed his session so much that he asked if he could do another hour. I agreed and he put on his clothes, darted to the ATM, and came back with more cash.

Despite the fact that Ishmael claimed he wouldn't have the courage to touch my breasts, he eventually did, and also asked if he could get a quick pussy peek, because again, he had never seen one in the flesh before...just the movies. His mouth opened and closed like a fish out of water when I folded down the front of my panties.

By the end of hour two, Ishmael was jerking off behind me and asking if I would bend over. Clearly his shyness had shrugged off rather quickly. And in two hours of pleasant conversation I had earned $280. Celebrate diversity!

72

A Price Even the Secret Service Wouldn't Haggle With

Recently, three of my clients claimed they'd previously patronized the masseuse next door to me—and she gives a release. After sharing a space with Gwen for months, a studio opened up downstairs in the same building. I signed a lease as quickly as possible.

I had my suspicions about Sally, the soft-spoken, married grandmother, who was your typical born-and-bred Coloradoan. She regales me with stories of when our now-burgeoning town was nothing more than farms and dirt roads, with the exception of a few paved roads.

She's hard-working and apparently gives both a great massage (she's a CMT) and hand job. When I originally moved into my spot, Sally was quite chatty, asking me all about my business. She mentioned that she, too, had almost all male clientele (clue #1). When I asked if the shower in our bathroom worked, she said it did, and that occasionally her clients have showered (clue #2!). Additionally, she doesn't bother with business cards in the reception area, a flashy website, or an attention-getting sign out front (ding, ding). Hmm… and she always seemed fairly busy. Granted, she's in her sixties, but I've heard many of the AMPs in town still employ seniors. And a guy can really picture whomever he wants when he closes his eyes with a woman's firm grip around his Johnson.

The only issue that had me on the fence was her fee: a mere $40 an hour, which is almost as low as you can go in this town, even without extras. I've been fascinated and a bit relieved by this revelation. Whereas I had to worry about the moans coming from my studio or the suspicious lack of even one female customer, I have no fear now. Seriously, this spot is perfect. But back to Sally.

Clients have told me that Sally kicks it old school by advertising in an actual paper; one of those free rags at the Feed-N-Grain. Can you believe it? An actual print publication? The literal equivalent of Backpage. Advertising this way would lead me to believe I'd end up with of bunch of men who feared that new-fangled thingamajig called the Internet. But in fact, I have scoped out Sally's clients, and they look fairly similar to my own. Men are like dogs when it comes to sniffing out an erotic masseuse. Particularly one that only charges a flat fee of $40 per hour; perhaps not cheap enough for those parsimonious Secret Service agents (seriously–$30 for double-dipped full-service?), but a frugal rate nonetheless.

The most recent client who mentioned seeing Sally said he paid $60 for an hour and a half massage.

"*And* she gives a hand job!" he said, wide-eyed.

"I've heard."

"She just throws that in for free," he claimed. "Maybe she just likes to stroke it."

Um, no.

Although my horror at Sally's bargain-basement prices might seem like I fear the competition, I don't. We are not offering the same thing. Men will pay more for the experience of fondling breasts and playing ass-grab for an hour, or having nipples skimmed down their back. Sally stays dressed in her ankle-length denim skirt and long-sleeved flannel. And then there is our age difference. Is the difference worth an $80 per hour premium? Apparently so, or those three clients would have booked with Sally instead of me.

One might think that Sally graciously charges $40 per hour, in the hopes that the client will make up the difference by tipping. I don't believe this is the case. The client who mentioned that she gave "free hand jobs" didn't mention giving her a tip. And I really don't think he did. If anything can be learned from the U.S. Secret Service prostitution scandal it's that negotiations should be upfront.

The thing that bothers me is that Sally is cleaning houses on the side to bring up her income, when she just needs to raise her prices to market value and skip that shit. If she's willing to give extras, she should be spending her days off lounging at the beauty parlor, not scrubbing toilets.

Even the AMPs around here charge $60 for a massage and a mandatory $60 tip. Sally might be older, but she can speak English fluently, Colorado-country accent notwithstanding, and she's Caucasian (that's a plus in the sex trade). She is also very pleasant and eager to please, according to her clients.

I'd like to give Sally a hint that she could bring up her prices. I'm guessing that she added the release option to her regular massages just to get the clientele, perhaps not realizing that she can charge a whole *lot* more. I doubt she woke up one morning and decided that she just couldn't keep her hands off cocks. Of course, bringing up this subject in a way that doesn't reveal what I do or put her on the defensive about what I think she's doing is touchy.

It's also possible that I'm horrified at Sally's rates because it foreshadows my future: I will consistently have to lower my prices just to stay busy. Seeing Sally daily as we pass each other in the hallway or waiting room is a reminder, a small nudge, if you will, like an ethereal voice in my head that tells me to *give up the money and find a way out* because I don't want to end up like Sally: still cashing in on my crumbling sexuality to pay the bills.

WINTER

73

MY NOT-SO-HAPPY ENDING

I had hoped that by the time I reached this point, I would be able to tell you that I had found a new job. One with decent pay, co-workers, benefits, and perhaps a coffee club. I would like to once again use the degrees (B.S., M.S.) I have earned.

No such luck. I look. I apply. And I wonder if I will ever again have some of the intellectually stimulating jobs I had before the recession.

I was also unable to sell my rental. I had just two showings the entire time it was on the market. I found new tenants and gave up on the notion of freeing myself from that financial liability. On a positive note, the mortgages are paid and my credit remains intact.

In the interim, as odd as it may sound, I'm glad to be an erotic masseuse. Even with part-time hours, I'm making more than $60,000 a year, which is a livable wage and typical compensation for what I do. One day, I looked down at all the cash I kept in a small suitcase and decided it was time to create a corporation so that I could deposit large amounts of cash in the bank, and report my income, without raising suspicions. I set myself up as an employee of my own company, which is a wise financial move on one hand and yet another example of how I am becoming more entrenched in my new identity on the other. I also renewed the lease on my latest studio, telling myself it would be easy to sublet—and I now take credit cards.

Besides the money, free time is another bonus of body rub work. I have ample time to pursue other interests, particularly ones that might yet yield a legal form of income. The sacrifices of being a body rub girl are forfeiting an honest and intimate relationship with a man and the burden of fabricating a double life to family and friends. Occasionally, I worry about getting arrested or outed. All these things are a great source of anxiety. I keep telling myself it's only temporary. It's been just over a year of sex work. Hopefully, it won't become my new career.

Or has it?